The Sales Chain

Robert Elliott

Tips, Tools, and an insider's view on the business of sales

Copyright © 2021 (Robert Elliott)
All rights reserved worldwide.

No part of the book may be copied or changed in any format, sold, or used in a way other than what is outlined in this book, under any circumstances, without the prior written permission of the publisher.

Publisher: Inspiring Publishers,
P.O. Box 159, Calwell, ACT Australia 2905
Email: publishaspg@gmail.com
http://www.inspiringpublishers.com

 A catalogue record for this book is available from the National Library of Australia

National Library of Australia The Prepublication Data Service

Author: Robert Elliott
Title: The Sales Chain
Genre: Non-fiction
ISBN: 978-1-922618-81-8

Disclaimer

The material in this book is of a general nature and comment and does not represent professional advice. It is not intended to be specific to any particular circumstance an should not be relied upon on any matter it covers to make any decision. Reader should always seek professional advice where appropriate before making any such decisions.

Contents

Dedication v
Meet the Author vii
My Sales journey ix

Introduction 1
1. Know who you are dealing with 5
   Engaging your client with Tony Ross 12
2. The Art of Listening 16
   Communication is the key with Alicia Sedgwick 21
3. Questions, Questions, Questions 25
4. What is a Niche? 30
5. Product Knowledge is not enough – 34
   Hunting Elephants and Closing Mega Deals
   with Peter Plaut 38
6. Objections- Bah Humbug 41
   Make your own luck in sales with Rob Doorey 46
7. Offer a Solution 50
8. Stories Sell 55
   The Art of Storytelling and Creating a Community
   with Tara Solberg 61
9. Tongue Tied 65
10. The Power of Social Media 71
11. The Most Important Word in Sales, NO! 78
12. Practice 83
13. Be your best self 87
    Mastering your stage with Adam Thompson 92
14. Attitude and Leadership 97
15. Virtual Selling 101
16. Close not Close 108
17. That's a Wrap 116

Dedication

> "To the people who believed in me
> when I did not believe in myself"

If we all take a moment to look back at our time on this earth, we would realise that we have been influenced by people and events without even knowing it.

I attended a high school where I felt I was a square peg in a round hole and never appreciated the lessons learned until many years later, and to that, I bow my head to my long-suffering teachers.

Post-school, I was, headstrong a poor listener, stubborn, and I am sure that many a boss called into a local bar on the way home in frustration of an employee who had the talent but was squandering it.

I owe everything I have achieved to my parents, who grew up working-class and shared a strong trait of determination, loyalty, and honesty. Mum and Dad were chalk and cheese in so many other ways.

Dad was a gentle soul who made everyone feel at ease and acknowledged, Mum was the straight shooter who didn't suffer fools and had a strong belief that there was no degree of perfection.

Even when big business threatened to take everything we had worked for away, they never flinched and fought to the very end.

Many of the lessons they taught me, I never realised until they both had passed, which is my regret. I was privileged to watch two people, both very different, be masters at sales without even realising it at the time.

My parents taught me the value of a customer, the importance of a quality product, and to respect the people that work with and for you.

Finally, to my beautiful wife, Rachel, who has picked me up many times when customers or life threatened to test my beliefs. I could never have achieved anything in life without her support, honesty and love.

My wish for you as you read this book is that you absorb some of the wisdom that my parents and others shared with me and implement it into your daily routine.

Meet the Author

Rob Elliott was born in Sydney, Australia, the only child of Jim and Cath Elliott. Rob's parents ran hotels, so he spent his childhood moving around Sydney. Rob attended five junior schools in his first six years of schooling.

School was never his forte, especially as he wore extra thick glasses due to being born with cataracts, as his Mum contracted Rubella when pregnant with him. Sadly, Rob bore the brunt of bullying during school, which only made him more resilient, he never let it hold him back from playing sport or doing things he loved.

After school, Rob worked a full-time job and also worked shifts behind the bar in his parent's hotel, ensuring a strong work ethic. Within a 12-month period, he met his wife of 32 years, Rachel, lost his mum to a heart attack, and sold the family business his father loved so much.

Rob and his wife moved to the outskirts of Sydney to raise their family. Being new to the area Rob threw himself into the local community. He had the privilege to be associated with some of the country's top business and political leaders, where he honed his craft for public speaking and fundraising for many charities. A proud Rotarian, Poppa to his beautiful granddaughter, skilled speaker, and trainer, he lives his life through the mantra;

"Just Be You"

My Sales Journey

If one could say you were born into sales, then I suppose that would be me. Growing up in the family business, my parents were hoteliers, I remember mum saying that everyone was in sales. People just don't realise it. I was too young to understand what she was trying to instil in me, and it was not until years later I understood that no matter who you are, or what line of work you do, we are all in sales, and yes, anyone can sell.

Behind the Bar in Australia

Working in a pub in Australia was a challenging place to learn how to sell, read body language and keep an aggressive, hard-to-please customer happy. My parents were experts in different ways at this, and I learned considerable from them. I learnt the skill of saying, no, while still making a customer feel as though they were the most important person in the room, ultimately it all came down to finding out what your customer wanted.

Sales is not just selling a product, it is as much about how you sell you, your ultimate product. I remember one night, when I was the only bar staff working and a customer had too much to drink and was being abusive. As I approached the customer, I realised immediately that he was taller, bigger and stronger than me. I took a deep breath and asked him to finish his drink, I knew he was sizing me up and could potentially hit me. I continued to stand my ground calmly, well calmly on the outside, watching his eyes as I knew that he could easily knock me out from where he stood.

For all intents and purposes, I may have been 10 feet tall. He looked me up and down, when he saw no response, he cursed and departed. I trusted that I did not need to watch my back. I believed that I was in charge, and I did not show any disrespect. I had learnt the art of the bluff and have used it many times during challenging sales negotiations.

You can Bank on that

Like all good sons, I took my parent's advice and accepted a job outside the business to gain additional skills in one of Australia's largest banks. Rows and rows of tellers writing in passbooks and endless paperwork for what seemed a minor transaction. I wasn't the right fit for the bank, I was the square peg in the round hole. I later found out that people who like sales suck at paperwork.

I did learn a lesson about how important things can be to people, and by doing just a small favour meant a lot to them. Little old ladies who waited in queue up to 30 minutes, before the bank opened to take their entire fortnightly pension out of the bank to buy their groceries and probably hide the remainder under the bed as they did not trust the banks to keep their money safe. Give them a new passbook cover or a money box to give their grandchild, and you automatically became the best teller on the line, till next week at least.

When your called to what you love

I knew that the bank and I just were not going to work, and potentially should part ways. I left to work for my Dad and his partner Bill in their bottle shop. I had always loved the liquor business, and it is where I felt most at home. The truth was, while I loved my job, I was the meat in the sandwich between two best mates who should have never gone into business together. It was evident that the three of us had very different ways of selling, which caused friction in the business.

This became my first encounter of having to manage different personalities.

I loved my position at the liquor store and when I was offered a job in the wholesale side of the industry, Dad then became my customer. My new boss was as popular with the customers as a broken egg in a new carton. She could not relate to clients, didn't listen to suggestions for improving processes and simply did not understand sales. I was later informed that the company had put her in the Manager's role as she did not get on with the office staff. After a prolonged period of my Manager being on extended leave, I approached her boss and said, my boss is not returning anytime soon, give me the opportunity take over, and I won't let you down. He agreed and I grew the business by 300%, reduced costs by 40%, and didn't drop our prices but provided exceptional customer service.

From there I moved into route sales with a large brewery, spirit supplier, and another broad range wholesaler. I was in charge of building a new business, rescuing declining sales, and working with leading brands which everybody thought was a cushy job, which was not so. The bigger the profile of a product, the bigger the expectations and demands to exceed targets.

Here I learnt the value of good branding, marketing, and advertising. Some product launches were fantastic, and others failed when product managers refused to entertain feedback from the sales team. I learned that exceptional leadership takes people on the journey, rather than just telling them what needs to be done like in management.

I had the pleasure of working for Guinness Australia, this is where I experienced what a great company culture was and how it reflected in results. We worked hard and achieved our targets and set outcomes. In return, Guinness rewarded us with complete support, acknowledgment, and a feeling of being part of a great organisation.

An industrial feel

All good things eventually come to an end, and I knew it was time for a change. For me sales are sales, it is only the product that is different. I dabbled in real estate sales while I was looking for the next challenge, I loved the actual selling side of it, but I found the lack of ethics by some agents, not all, very disappointing.

I was given the opportunity to go back to basics and do the door-to-door side in the industrial sphere, hard work at the best of times, with a tough clientele and even more competitive markets. The work paid off, and I was soon running a team of salespeople and being thrown a $5 million account that had only been with the company for 6 months that was about to walk with the brief to save the account and you will save your job. Well, it took another six months, but I maintained the account, grew the sales bottom line, and enjoyed watching my team grow professionally and personally. At this company, I learnt that honesty is always the best policy, you never know what your customer knows and to build trust, you must be honest, even if it hurts.

Industrial markets are challenging, and no matter if you are selling gas, concrete, or a pair of boots, people are really all just the same. Most only treat you as they have been treated in the past, so creating lasting change takes time and patience.

Using your skill for good

Raising funds for charity can be a real challenge, especially when you are competing for people's money and respect. You only get a short window to build trust, and people expect a higher level of transparency when they are donating their money and need to know, to whom and where their money is going.

My wife, Rachel, and I decided early on that if we could help those in need, we would use our skills and contacts to make a difference. I am proud to say we have both raised many thousands of dollars for causes and charities that we believe in.

When raising funds for charities, you need to do it for ones that you genuinely believe in. If you don't, you will hurt your reputation and the charity you are doing it for. Everything here is based on trust, and people who give you their money must trust you.

I have been blessed with the ability to obtain money out of just about anyone for a cause I believe in, never have I allowed anyone to give more than they can afford, and I always show genuine gratitude. It is immensely rewarding when you meet someone, who has benefited from what you have done, and says thank you with a tear in their eye, this is truly priceless.

Should we ever meet in person, beware if you find yourself with my arm around your shoulder, and I ask can you spare me five minutes. I guarantee that both of us will come away with a smile and one with a much lighter wallet in the name of a good cause.

I hope you enjoy reading about my journey and the lessons I have learnt as you build your own Sale Journey.

Introduction

So many people I speak to, say they cannot sell and are terrified of the thought, yet they have been selling all their life without knowing it.

The best salespeople usually go unnoticed and quietly go about their business without much fanfare. Close your eyes, and think about your school days or early adulthood and the kid who was always popular in school or the person who got all the attention at the bar on a Friday night. Once you open your eyes, it is easy to see that they already knew how to sell themselves. Everyone has done this from time to time, got a bit more sauce on their pie, been recommended a better fragrance at the store, or even got a date from someone they admired across a room. Yes, that is right, all these acts are just selling yourself, and you never realised it.

This book is all about sharing stories, skills, and tactics to help those who want to improve their selling skills or want to improve their confidence to succeed in their current role. There is no secret ingredient or special steps that guarantee 100% success in selling, even though many on social media will try and tell you otherwise. Selling is just like any other skill, it takes practice, hard work, and belief in what you are doing to succeed.

Just like learning how to play a sport, you will crash and burn, miss an opportunity or two, and even stuff up along the way. More importantly, by the end of this book, you will grow from a place of not knowing what went wrong to identifying and pivoting to improve your success.

There will also be times when you do everything right, and nothing comes out of it that you see. Wrong, I believe in two things, one Everything happens for a reason and two Everything happens for us, not to us. In other words, no matter the result, there is something always to be learnt and to grow from and it will not reveal itself until it is ready.

This book will also help those who are not directly involved in sales, but whose actions can substantially impact a sale happening or even continuing. Many companies only provide training to front-line sales staff and ignore everyone else, a fatal mistake. The whole process is just like a chain, and you know what happens if you have a weak link.

I have been blessed to have some great mentors along the way in my 30 plus years of sales and helping others in the skill of selling. My mum and dad allowed me to watch, learn, create my own path, and see the value of relationship selling in industry. I believe there is not a mistake I have not made along the way while I have worked in some of Australia's most competitive industries and companies, yet those same challenges taught me so much.

From a very young age, I was told I could sell anything to anyone, and yes, I have been blessed with confidence from my parents and knowledge from great and not-so-great bosses to be able to do just that.

Watching those who sold just for the single sale and those who built long-term relationships taught me much along the way. How we deal and interact has evolved hugely, yet the principles behind what we do have not changed that much, only how we deliver them.

Later, I will share real case studies that will highlight some of the skills we are discussing. There are also contributions from sales professionals from around the world, who are experts in their respective fields. They will share their own experiences and pearls of wisdom.

Finally, I ask you not to wait to finish this book before using the strategies you learn. Try them out every day and see how you go. Remember, everyone is different, and the one thing that I ask you as a hard rule is that You just be You! People can pick a fake in 30 seconds or less.

Enjoy the book, and remember,

Have a Groovy Day!

Bonus material

**For additional resources,
and to access Rob Elliotts podcast
and special offers please visit
www.robelliott.com.au**

Chapter One

Know who you are dealing with

Before we start, you need to understand the four traits of people that you will interact with each day. Most people are a mix of two traits, with one trait more dominant than the other.

When you understand your customer, it will be easier to address their needs and increase the chance of a sale.

In nearly all cases you can assess and identify a person's traits within a few minutes of your initial meeting. By observing their body language, listening to them talk, and the intent in their delivery you will pick up the style of person you are dealing with.

At all times you need to be willing to adapt and pivot as most people have a combination of each trait. If you choose to interact with a customer in just one manner and they react adversely, it is because you engaged in a way, they were uncomfortable with.

I recommend a cautious approach until you are confident in reading people. Remember this is not about changing who you are but understanding who you are interacting with.

Types of People

Have you ever questioned why you have instant rapport with some people and not with others? And regardless of how hard you try; you simply don't connect. This is because there are three ways people process their surroundings. These are called modalities; it is how we see the world using our senses.

It is easy to build rapport with someone who uses the same modality as the one you regularly use. The skill is to identify which one your customer uses and to mirror it.

Here is a short guide to the three senses most used

Sight – Visual, Sound – Auditory, Touch- Kinaesthetic

A Visual person will frequently use the below words when talking and replying to questions.

Brilliant, Paint a Picture, Look, View, Focus, Reveal, Show

An Auditory person will use the words below when talking and answering questions

Announce, Hear, Be All Ears, Clear as a Bell, on another note, it rings a Bell.

A Kinaesthetic person will use the words below when talking and answering questions.

Grasp, Solid, Catch on, Touch point, Texture, Soft, Firm, Smooth

People use a mixture of all three, but they will have a dominant style, which you can emulate.

The Process Customer

For a person in sales, processes are viewed as the ultimate hand brake to achieving their targets or budgets. Truthfully, we all need process to ensure success.

The administrator who asserts that your order cannot be processed as you haven't followed due process, can be seen as the handbrake. But for them it is the correct way to move forward and we [the sales guru's] need to acknowledge it.

In sales, a process driven client is that way because it makes them feel in control, when they are following a procedure. Without individuals who implement and apply processes and systems, little would be achieved and we [the sales guru's] would not have rules to bend.

Process people are analytical, exact, very formal, quiet and do not give much away. They appreciate being given precise information in a detailed, direct, and patient manner. If you apply pressure for an immediate response, they will retreat.

The best method to communicate with process customers is to focus on the quality of the information, talk logically and methodically, explaining nuisances. Allow the customer time to absorb the information, ask if there are any questions or areas that they would like to be expanded upon.

It is important to remember with this process driven customer, that you need to stay in the business lane, no frivolous comments, like where you had dinner last night.

The Direct Customer

At some time, we have all encountered this person. Possibly, you have a relative or friend who is quite direct and makes for an interesting dinner guest and discussion.

Direct customers are an absolute joy to deal with when you are having a tough day, said no one ever. They are known for being extremely direct with their comments, some can be impatient, demanding, and seldom listen to what you are trying to tell them. You can easily derail the interaction by trying to elaborate, as this will elicit the belief that you are slowing the process or threatening the customer's position of power. Do not, and I repeat do not spend time on information or activities that do not directly involve or interest them. Trust me my wife falls into this category, and I know from years of experience that this can be a bad move.

However, when given direct feedback and the validation that you are focusing on the result they wish to achieve, they will and do respond.

Communicating with them can be hit and miss, bit like the weather bureau predicting the 5 day forecast. You never can really rely on, the information at hand as a direct person can be like the weather, unpredictable. However, all is not lost, if you give them their space and stick to the task at hand, they will respond quite quickly. Always provide a solution that makes them feel empowered and validated.

When you make them feel good, they tend to decide quickly. So, load them up with all the facts, feedback, and solutions until they wane under your vast knowledge, being none the wiser.

The Chilled-out Customer

When it has been a tough day, it's always a pleasure to come across a customer like this. They have their uniqueness, but generally, they are very caring, patient people who take the time to listen carefully to what you are saying.

They come across as a trustworthy and humble person who can also be indecisive, which will frustrate even the best salespeople. In general, you must balance giving them time to respond and decide without pressure. Always, always deliver what you promised. Failure here can be fatal.

Communication can be a marathon with customers like this. They need to feel included, and their opinion valued and incorporated into any response, which logically, shows how the solution benefits them. Without their input, there will be no sale.

I recommend taking a step-by-step approach, seeking agreement at each stage, as this removes the ability to be blindsided later and ensures they feel part of the planning. This will also expose any extra information you may need.

The key to success with this client is to slow down, relax and allow time for discussion, this will build trust and secure commitment.

The Excited Customer

It does not matter what industry you work in; these customer's energy can be so infectious that it is dangerous. Yes, they have a single ability to derail everything we know and have learnt as we try to match their energy level.

They are sociable, spontaneous and can talk under water. Being detailed or focused is not normally a trait associated with them. Instead, emotion and impulsiveness lead their decision-making process, which they tend to justify with some form of logic later.

It is best in the moment to hang on for the ride, smile, and remain positive, as any indication of negativity or not matching their enthusiasm can and will derail the train.

Communicating with these customers can be described as riding the Californian Screaming Roller coaster at Disneyland, it only goes one speed, flat out. The best approach is to acknowledge the feelings they are expressing, stay accessible and always keep smiling.

They will talk about everything else than what you are there for, then they will redivert back onto topic with rapid-fire questions expecting quick responses.

There is nothing more to do, but sit back and enjoy the experience, as you are the subject matter expert and know your product inside out. Make them feel relaxed and happy and all will be fine well.

Key Takeaways

Chilled Out Customers
Do take your time, be patient, chill, and smile.
Do not rush, pressure, or fail to deliver.

The Process Customer
Do be detailed, relaxed, flexible.
Do not be impatient, general, unfocused.

The Excite Customer
Do always be positive, fun, friendly.
Do not be too detailed, negative, quiet.

The Direct Customer
Do remain focused on the subject, result/solution orientated.
Do not challenge, be flippant, emotional.

Case Study

This is not what I asked for

I remember the first time I was asked to assist in writing a radio advertisement. We worked hard focusing on our target audience, incorporating as many styles as possible, using the information we have covered in this chapter.

We forwarded our brief to the radio station, which outlined the style of voice and words we wanted used to cover the targeted demographic.

If you listen to politicians and radio advertisements on different radio networks you will have noticed that even if the message is the same, the delivery is based on the audience: words, tone, speed, all change based on the demographic. Most of the time we miss these subtle differences, but they do make a huge difference to the result.

While we acknowledged we couldn't cover all styles, we were confident we had nailed it. On hearing the first audio draft of the advertisement, it was the complete opposite to our detailed brief, even wording had been changed. In fact, it did not match what we wanted at all and when I questioned them, I was informed that the person we requested to create our advertisement was not available, so they simply improvised.

They had failed to read the customer we were pitching to and had potentially destroyed our campaign if we moved forward. We had it changed and it ended up being a very successful campaign.

Sidenote: I never used that radio station again.

Engaging your client with - Tony Ross

Short Biography

A Financial Services Industry veteran with almost forty years' experience ranging from Sales Management to self-employed Practice Manager and Owner. Tony is now a semi-retired Senior Strategist. Tony worked through some of the most tumultuous times that the financial services industry could imagine, during all of this he continued to be recognised for his achievements in running and owning a multi-award-winning business. In 2016 Tony was recognised by the Asia Pacific Financial Services Association as a Fellow Chartered Financial Practitioner and in 2020 sold his business to explore new opportunities.

In his spare time Tony primarily seeks to spend time with family and friends but continues to involve himself in his local community. Tony is currently the Chairman of Lifeline Macarthur and Western Sydney and has served 15 years on the Board of Youth Solutions including three years as President.

It's all about the Engagement

There is no doubt that the Financial Services industry has seen change on a massive scale over the past 20 years or so and the pace seems to be accelerating as more and more emphasis is placed on compliance with regulations and oversight. The era of caveat emptor (let the buyer beware) is long dead and we should be eternally grateful for that because it has forced professional salespeople, particularly in the services arena but not exclusively, to consider their obligations to their prospective and existing customers and to focus upon building a relationship of trust and reliability that can sustain a longer term and probably more fruitful relationship with clients who are willing to engage. The focus of the successful professional has moved to the engaged relationship of mutual benefit and away from the "wham, bam, make the sale, Sam" mentality that was for too long the way business was done.

So, what exactly is this engaged relationship? From a Financial Services perspective, the engaged relationship begins with the establishment of a very clear understanding of what the client is seeking to achieve and what issues they need to consider as a part of their journey, (including the issues that they have either not thought of or don't know about). In setting the scene for this I often discussed with clients my experiences during the Sydney Olympics. I had decided that I would attend sports that I had not previously considered, and Archery was one that appealed. Many Australians would remember a young Australian named Simon Fairweather who won Gold at the Sydney Olympics. I was over the moon to watch his performance during the games however the professional side of me looked at how the sport was run and realised that if they removed the target, it would be simply a group of people seeing how far they could send their projectile. The whole point of Archery is having a clear and visible target to aim at and, most importantly, understanding what represents a win (a bullseye if you will). So clear targets and a vision of success are a critical starting point and must be provided by the client and understood by their adviser.

Once you are on the same page in terms of the preferred outcome, the next step is to understand where the client will be starting from. This is also critical to the engagement piece because it goes far beyond the client's financial position, the professional salesperson will explore the clients understanding and experience, their fears and concerns and promote a robust discussion around issues that they have not considered but need to. In Financial Services, the best example of this is a discussion around Insurance - there is no point trying to build wealth if you do not protect it from misfortune through death or ill-health and most clients understand this (they don't like insurance, and its cost, but recognise its importance) but what they often forget is the inclusion of a discussion around their estate planning (will, etc.) to make sure that the money goes to the right person quickly should the worst happen. Building an engaged relationship is a lot easier if you as the professional salesman can help them to cover all bases that are necessary and can lead to additional revenue for you (would you like fries with that anyone).

The next step in building an engaged relationship is the critical point, everything to date has been building to this point, the sale! By now you have established a clear target for the client to achieve, you have ascertained where your client is starting from and established all the relevant issues and side considerations and had a robust discussion with the client not only about their importance but also about whether they are to be included in your considerations. All you need know is the pitch, the display of your professional skills, knowledge and experience that will provide the solution that your client requires.

The key to your pitch is relating back to everything your client has revealed and providing an outcome with clear victories, benefits and alignment to the client's goals - really, how can your client say no, if you have addressed the very targets that you have drawn from them, and, frankly, if they do, you must ask whether or not this is the client for you anyway. Obviously, it is a little more complicated than this, but the fundamental message remains the same - if you are solving the problem that the clients want solved, it will be straightforward to close the sale.

Finally, don't forget we are looking for an engaged relationship rather than just a one-off sale so set landmarks that will require reviews and adjustments. Remind the client that things change and may need re-assessment and establish the basis for regular reviews to monitor their position as well as the cost of these reviews and how they can add value to the client's journey to success.

So, there you have the framework for building engaged relationship with your client, but the fact is that none of this will work if you are not engaged yourself. If you don't clearly demonstrate the value, you can add and the commitment you have, why should your client engage with you. I will close these musings with some advice my father gave me as I set out on this journey all those years ago, treat people as you would like them to treat you, work hard for them and they will see it, be trustworthy and reliable and you will become invaluable. I can attest to this and will add one more thing for you to consider - you will also become successful!

Chapter Summary/Key Takeaways

1. The key to longer term success in sales is the relationship you build with your clients.
2. Engagement is the key.
3. Understanding the client goals and objectives, educating them on issues that they need to address and drawing them to outline what they want is the foundation.
4. Providing a solution that is clearly aligned with their targets, demonstrates this and shows specific benefits, advantages and wins is all the closing you need.
5. Building a long term engaged (and commercial) relationship needs checkpoints.
6. How you choose to engage with your clients should align with how you would like them to engage with you - put their best interests first always and obviously.

Chapter Two

The Art of Listening

It does not matter who you speak to in sales today, anyone who has been successful will tell you that the essential key is the ability to listen. A person will always divulge more than you have asked. It is essential that you are tuned in to hear what is being said.

This chapter will cover the different forms of listening; active listening, attentive listening, and listening with your eyes. While the percentages are debated, most people acknowledge that communication is 80% non-verbal and 20% verbal. When we communicate, we can pick up on the signals, spoken word, and subtle hints our clients do during our interactions.

Active Listening

We have two ears and one mouth, yet a lot of people do not use them in that sequence. Active listening gives you the opportunity to learn everything you need to know from your customer by simply responding to what is being said to you which in turn results in mutual understanding. When we actively listen, we put ourselves in the best position to answer all the questions being asked and reduce the likelihood of missing key facts.

A customer is made to feel important when they believe they have been listened to, acknowledged and a solution to their needs provided.

That does not mean that you agree with everything they have said, but at least they know you have heard them. I call it being fully present in coaching, with no distractions and complete focus on what is being said.

Always be 100% present for your client or customer. It does not matter if you only interact with them for a short period, during that time, it can feel like longer if they believe you are not giving them your full attention.

I was at our local hardware store buying paint and waiting in the queue to pay. The cashier was distracted and looking the other way. I approached and said "Hello, how's your day" she glanced back at me started to scan my items, still looking at what was being said up the line. The cashier never once answered or paid any attention to the task at hand. In the end, I said, "I suppose what is going on up there is more important than looking after me" I received a blank look back, "and by the way, you have charged me twice for the paint". The cashier sheepishly called the supervisor over and had the overcharge amended.

I don't blame the cashier as I don't believe they had been properly trained in customer service. Nevertheless, it could have been avoided by them taking the time to acknowledge the customer, focus on what they were doing, and I would have left a happy customer. There would not have been the need for the staff member to explain to their supervisor how the overcharge occurred.

Acknowledging your client, or practicing Attentive Listening, doesn't mean agreeing with them. There is nothing more annoying than having a conversation with another person, and you receive zero feedback, you find yourself in a position of not knowing if you have been heard, misunderstood or ignored.

The same theory applies when you are communicating with a customer. A simple acknowledgment of yes, head nod, or repeating an abridged version of what they have said works wonders, especially when building rapport with new clients.

Have you ever spoken to a young child or student who gives you an answer nowhere near what you have asked them? They were hearing you to respond, not listening to hear you. A simple response that is relevant to what the customer has said will make all the difference. This provides an acknowledgment and the affirmation that you were paying attention.

Some people fear asking questions of a client as they feel it makes them look inferior. You should never be afraid of giving your customer the best option or solution, and if asking a question does that, then go for it. For example, you own a Fish'n'Chip shop, your customer purchases fries with salt, and you assume that they want plain salt. When the order is ready, they ask do you have chicken salt oops, you look bad, fries are wasted, profit margins are impacted and one unhappy customer.

This may seem simple but asking questions can open up an extra sale and identify an opportunity to upsell or add on. It comes down to the delivery of the question that makes your client feel important. By checking in with them you can avert a mistake and deliver for your client. Remember the old adage 'do you want fries with that?

Going Deep

Sometimes in important negotiations or emotional purchases you will be required to listen what we call "Deeply". Meaning you need to pay closer attention to what's not being said, much like when your partner is yelling at you.

Concentrate on distinctive words that have not been used before and use silence to bring out more information as your client battles to communicate what they want to say as their emotions take hold.

If you feel your client needs prompting then ask them a soft question about themself or what they are doing, then go quiet and listen with every bone of your body and they will reveal what the real story is.

When you listen deeply you will hear their motivations and see the world through their eyes. This will enable you to truly serve them and provide exactly what they need.

Taking Notes

This one is for account managers/sales reps when dealing with more significant sales but it can also be used in retail when customers have a long list of requests.

Notes serve two purposes; one, a form of acknowledgment that your client knows you are taking a genuine interest in what they are saying, and secondly, it ensures you do not miss anything and have a reference for all requests. Taking notes saved me on numerous occasions and removed the need to make a return call to ask a question about about topics already discussed.

Listening with your Eyes

Listening with your eyes or as it is more commonly known, body language, is an important skill to master. It provides you with additional information about your client, without having to say one word. A person's demeanour, stance, gestures, tone, pitch, and manner are all indicators for what they are feeling and thinking.

Unless someone has undertaken training to master their body language, they will always freely provide you with information about what they are thinking. A cross of the arms, the touch of their face, or the disengage of eye contact are all traits that provide nonverbal cues and are vital when you are selling.

Play this game at home with a child or relative. Ask them three questions that you know will extract a positive response, watch their body language, then ask them a question that makes them feel uncomfortable, or that you know they will answer negatively.

When you practice actively observing people, it will become natural for you to notice the signals given by a client. Even with the most challenging client, who is giving nothing away verbally, you will know by their reaction, when asked a question where the interaction is headed.

If you propose something to a client and they shift in their seat, pause, frown, or anything you sense is negative, go ahead and ask them if there is a concern or if there is information that needs clarification. There is no problem asking a targeted question.

Key Takeaways

What makes a good listener?
- Be 100% there for your client.
- Respond and acknowledge what is being said.
- Do not be afraid to ask questions to clarify.
- Never interrupt. Wait until they have finished talking.
- Notice your clients' words, tone, and pitch.
- Notice your client's body language.
- Do not listen to respond.
- Ensure your body language is open and relaxed.

What makes a poor listener?
- Doesn't pay attention, is distracted.
- Is actively waiting to respond before hearing the whole story.
- Interrupts.
- Closed body language.
- Fails to acknowledge a client's position before answering with a suggestion.
- Assumes rather than checking the facts.
- Rushes the client.

"Confidence is silent, insecurities are loud"
Ryan Serhant
Million Dollar Listing New York

Communication is the key with - ALICIA SEDGWICK

Alicia Sedgwick is a Communication Coach, Corporate Trainer, Author and professional MC based in Monte Carlo, Monaco, with an extensive background in the Entertainment and Events Industry.

Her first book "Communicating Through Change" became an overnight international bestseller upon its launch in January 2021.

She teaches at the International University of Monaco as well as offering private coaching to Corporations, Associations, International Schools, Foundations and individuals.

A City Trained lawyer, Alicia has hosted three Tedx Conferences, managed International Press Conferences for the London 2012 Olympics, and Managed red carpets for the Laureus World Sports Awards. She has Managed Talent Relations for the BBC Chelsea Flower Show in London, and in the "Green Room" of the World Music Awards. In 2021, Alicia co-curated Monaco's first TEDx Youth Event held at the International School of Monaco.

A professional blues singer and stage performer for over 25 years, Alicia has hosted her own Internet TV Show, and Radio Show.

Communicating Through Sales

Success in your career depends on how you speak, write and think.... in that order. Why? Because nobody knows what you think until you speak or write. Effective communication is what distinguishes the successful professional from everyone else in today's competitive environment. For Sales, as other careers, it is all about how you relate to your clients and customers, and how you present yourself through your speaking and writing – how you communicate.

When we use the word "communicate", we are referring not only to words that are used to transfer factual information to another, but also to other "messages" that are sent or received.

It is through words, actions, body language, tone of voice, and other processes that you send many messages about yourself, about your organisation, and the product that you are selling. This is precisely half of the communication process. The second half is to verify that your message is received and interpreted in the way you intended it to be. Here's a few tips on how to achieve effective communication.

1. Adapt your communication style to your audience. Know your audience. Any presentation that you make is never about you. It is about your audience – what is that you want them to think, feel or do as a result of your communication? Every person you talk to or sell to has different motivations so knowing how to tailor your communication is essential to influencing others and reaching your goals and targets.
2. Use multiple communication channels. There are many ways to communicate with your clients or customers. Since individual clients will respond better to different methods than others, be sure not to rely on a singular channel. These can include one-on-one's, emails, videos, social media.
3. Be clear. Always speak in specifics. Clearly define the product, the opportunities, and benefits if bought or used by your client, and about what you want to see achieved and can be achieved for the recipient of your sales.

4. Keep an open body language. Communication isn't just what you say. More than ninety-three percent of communication's impact comes from nonverbal cues. Positive body language supports your points, helps you convey ideas more clearly, and avoids sending mixed messages. Good posture, good eye contact, good Zoom technique count!
5. Be Transparent. By speaking openly about the challenges as well as the opportunities for the client, you will build trust amongst your customers and foster an environment where all clients feel empowered to share their ideas, collaborate and be continuing clients.
6. Practice empathy. The better you get at acknowledging and understanding your client's needs, the more heard and valued they will feel, and, again, they will be loyal and stay with you for many years.
7. Actively listen to the people with whom you communicate. Remember that, although you communicate in a way that seems clear to you, the recipient of the message has their own information "filters" which can distort the message received.
8. Do not be afraid to get feedback. Receivers of your message have selective listening: they hear and process certain information and neglect others. The only way to make sure you've created a common understanding is to ask others what they heard and what their reactions are.

And finally.... get help! Admit it if you are not another Tony Robbins and you need professional communications training. An effective salesperson is someone who inspires and empowers those around them to buy the product or close the deal. When good communication skills are lacking, important information can be misinterpreted, causing relationships to suffer and, ultimately, creating barriers that hinder progress. Communication skills, like all skills, need to change and adapt to current needs. Embrace the need for learning how to effectively communicate in your work.

Chapter Summary/Key Takeaways

Effective communication is key in Sales! It is more than just the way you speak. This chapter gives some tips on how you can develop your communication skills. Most of all, be clear, be observant, listen and know that it is never about you – it is always about your client and customer and what you want them to think, feel or do as a result of your communication with them.

Chapter Three

Questions, Questions, Questions,

Questions asked correctly, at the right time are essential to every sale conversation. They must be asked with genuine interest, and you need to actively listen when a response is given. We have all experienced the call centre operator asking us a range of questions. You can visualise them deciding what to ask next based on your reply, so phoney, disingenuous, yet effective in their situation.

Having a process or list of questions to gain the information you need as quickly as possible is not necessarily a bad thing, especially when you are first starting out or dealing with a technical product. It beats having to call someone back to ask a question you should have known to ask at the first contact, embarrassing.

There are, however, many different types of questions, and knowing what type to use and when is essential.

Open Questions

Open questions are my favourite type as they start a discussion and provide the information you need to delve further. These questions cannot be answered with a simple yes or no. It typically takes three open questions before you get to the real issue a client has. Examples could be, "How did you come to choose that product", or "What is it you like about this house". They allow the client to respond in the way they feel comfortable.

Leading Questions

Leading questions are specifically designed to elicit the response that you are looking for. It is a great way to highlight the positives of your product and move your client into a positive state. These questions can highlight negative points around an alternate offer if you take it back to a positive end. Great to use when you want to close a deal off as people enjoy saying yes rather than no. Ask your client, "That is a magnificent view, isn't it" or "I noticed you enjoyed the ride in our new model. What did you like the most?" Finalising a conversation with a positive exchange is the optimal way to close a sale.

Closed Questions

I believe every adult has been on the end of an answer from a young child when asking these questions and get the short response or "Yes or No". These questions are perfect when a quick or focused response is required, "How was your day?" "Did you get the train here?" "Have I covered everything". More often than not, a closed question will lead to an open question, and as a rule, avoid asking three closed questions in a row as it can come off as being uninterested. Closed questions do help at the end of a negotiation to acknowledge the points covered to clarify the discussion. Like a short summary.

Asked and Answered Questions

These questions are typically used during a live presentation to a group or when a salesperson feels very confident about a client. Put simply, it is asking a question and implying the answer in the same sentence. This works two-fold as it reinforces the presenter's opinion and leads the client to answer the way, the presenter suggests.

By saying "You would have to agree that what we are offering you today is a great deal" or "Your delivery driver is certainly on his game". You can frame any positive statement into one of these styles of questions to build engagement and create rapport when first meeting a new prospect or moving to close a deal.

Clarification Questions

There comes a time during all sales conversations that you need to dig deeper to get the real story behind your client's motivation. These questions should be specific around crucial information you need to service your client and ensure you provide what they need. Ask questions like "When are you looking to build" or "What is the most essential feature you need in this computer". You can use any style of the question here as long as you avoid misunderstandings and extract vital clues about who your competition is.

Asking the Question, that you already know the answer to

Have you ever felt that a person asking you questions already knows the answer? The first lesson I learnt as a young salesperson was never to ask a question that you didn't already know the answer to. Do not ask a question that you know will provide a negative response. Of course it is fine to ask a question to seek confirmation of what you know is valid for clarity but steer clear of anything that may derail the sale.

Emotional Questions

Feelings, nothing more than feelings Yes, we have all heard the line and asking questions that elicit positive emotions is always beneficial. People buy emotionally and justify later, so what is wrong with putting your client in an emotional state that makes them feel good. "How good are you going to look in that suit", "What will it mean to your family to move into a larger home". Any statement framed as an emotional question is a potent tool and can close a deal then and there.

Why never ask Why!

The most straightforward question to ask anyone is why they did something or why you said that. If you want a truthful answer, then never ask any question with a why. This is because asking this way prompts what we call "Justification Mode" in people. They automatically think they need to justify why they did something, and their mind starts looking for excuses around their decision.

When you are seeking a response around a decision, ask "What made you come to that decision" or "How did you come to that decision". Test it on your kids next time they do something that makes you displeased, you will get the answer you need, not the one they want to give you.

Key Takeaways

The beauty of asking questions is that it brings you knowledge that you can use to move a deal forward or back. Never be afraid to ask as many as you feel that is necessary to and be confident to ask the most important one. Is that a Deal?

- Open questions lead to more questions.
- Leading questions go where you want them to go.
- Closed questions give you certainty.
- Ask & Answered questions bring agreeance.
- Clarification questions bring focus.
- Never ask a question you may not like the answer to.
- Emotions move a client to buy.

Chapter Four

What is a Niche?

Let's get this straight: A niche is not a French dessert; a niche is your target market. It covers both product and your customer. It is defined by where you intend to sell your service or product. The benefit you provide will fill the needs and wants for your intended market.

If you fail to understand your market, there will be missed opportunities to generate leads and increase sales. For example, identifying if it is appropriate to sell jumpers at a market store in Perth at the height of summer is understanding your market, alternately ensuring you have both male and female staff available to look after customers in a culturally diverse community can be the difference between success and failure.

When it comes to sales, knowing your niche is critical to success. Without it, a company or person can be labelled as using a scattergun approach. For example, a company is releasing a product to the whole market, in the hope they buy it, a saleperson in person-to-person sales decides to call everyone in the phone book and hope they are interested in buying. This may work short-term, but sales decline rapidly as other companies enter the market with a more targeted marketing approach.

Have you ever noticed a person being more comfortable talking to one demographic of people than others? This is because they are more comfortable and relaxed around people who appear to share the same interests and values.

It is true that people buy people. When you create a niche that you are comfortable working in, you will attract those same people and have more success, you will glow with confidence in their presence, and they, in turn, will be more comfortable working with you.

The same is said about products or businesses. Have you ever heard someone say that XZY Laptops have a reputation as the best in video production. The company identified a potential market and targeted that area with specific marketing and quality products until people knew them as the expert in their area. People who work in real estate use the same strategy, so they become known as area experts or prestige homes specialists. They continue to build confidence and reputation around their niche and customers seek them out.

How do you identify your Niche?

Identifying your niche is necessary to ensure success and should be reviewed at least every twelve months and when the market has a significant shift in customer focus.

The following questions will assist to identify your target market.

What is the most popular age group for my product or service? e.g., 30-40 demographic. This information is vital as it will assist with how and where you market your product or service.

Are you more at ease dealing with Male or Females?

Is the product or service relevant to Male / Females or both?

Is your ideal customer in a specific trade or business? This is a general question and can be modified to suit your skill.

Who needs your skills/service the most?

What does your product have that your competitor's don't? What is your unique selling point?

Where does your ideal customer go to find out information?

The purpose of these questions is to understand what will attract a customer to your business. Your research may identify that it is not feasible to enter a specific market and may require adjustments to your business. This will enable you to tailor your message to suit your ideal client.

By going through this process, there is the potential to identify new markets or areas that you and your business may need to improve. Regardless, it will be a win.

Can you have more than one Niche?

Many companies market the same product or service to different demographics but utilise alternate and differing styles of marketing strategies dependent on who the target is. There is nothing wrong with having more than one niche, as it is unwise to walk away from potential success. It may just take a little more persistence to win.

How to reach your target Market

Regardless of size or experience, you will face uncertainty when beginning your marketing plan. By identifying your potential client through research, you will know where your client shops. This will reveal their influences and the ideal location for your advertisements to ensure optimal traction.

It would be pertinent to test a few market areas and analyse the rate of response and return. Analysing this data will offer solutions and feedback to ensure you offer a solution, not just a product.

Key Takeaways

- Know what you have to offer.
- Identify who needs your service and product.
- Become part of their community.
- Offer value and service.
- Be the solution your client needs.
- Know where you are most comfortable, as that is where you will sell the most.

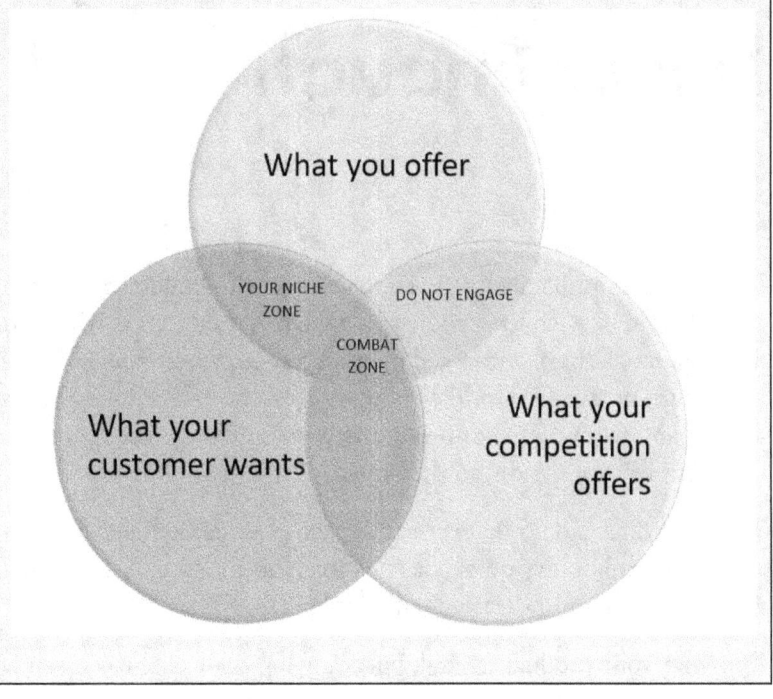

Chapter Five

Product Knowledge Is Not Enough

It is a common mistake made by managers who believe that if they train their staff with the product knowledge, then that is where the training ends. I have witnessed many instances where they overload their team or train them like robots to disseminate information at a hasty and fast rate to confuse a customer and wear them down to the point of submission, so they buy.

The other downside is that the staff get so preoccupied they blurt out all the information as quickly as possible and forget to listen, and as we know, failing to hear is a fatal flaw in sales.

Knowing your product is vital, but knowing your client is essential even if you have only just met them. You will hear me say many times that "People buy People," which is the best motto anyone in sales can live by.

A customer does not have to like you, or you like them, but if they feel respected and are confident in what you are saying, they will put aside their feelings and buy.

The best way to teach this subject is with the following case study, which highlights the importance of knowing your product while also valuing the customer.

Case Study: How Not to Sell a Mobile Phone

Not so long ago, I needed to replace my aging mobile phone as it was starting to show signs of slowing, and I was prophesying seeing the black screen of death at any time. I have a preferred brand and have been with the same provider for over ten years, so while I was out shopping, I thought I would pop into one of their branded stores to see my options as I was now out of contract and ready to buy.

The store was very well presented with the brands they want you to buy at the front and plenty of staff eager to answer your questions (reach sales target). I looked around and saw three versions of the same brand of phone and thought I would enquire what the difference was and cost.

It went downhill from that point on. The salesperson I approached led with his usual, what plan are you on? I told him, and then I asked about the difference between the phones. His eyes lit up, and for the next, it seemed forever; he proceeded to tell me the ins and outs of all three phones, the different plans, and what I should use. Sounds ok so far, but he had made some fatal mistakes.

For the majority of our interaction, he looked straight out the front of the store at the passing shoppers, occasionally glancing back briefly only to return his focus to what was around us. He never asked if I was ready to buy a phone today, what I use my phone for, was my contract still in place, or if I had any special requirements.

During this I stayed quiet as he rattled off the camera, storage, and colors available, I was still not being asked even the simplest of questions.

I left the store without a phone, I was probably not the only sale, to walk out the door. I walked around to their competition to see what they had on offer.

Well, you guessed right, I did buy a new phone but not with my preferred store, I got a better deal with an upgraded product, and will never go back to that site or recommend it to anyone else again.

The experience reminded me of an interview with Alicia Sedgwick, a communications expert living in France who teaches at the International University in Monaco. Alicia spoke about how hospitality companies spend millions of dollars on branding, advertising, store layouts. It can all be worth nothing if the delivery of the waiter or salesperson in the store is inadequate.

You can have all the knowledge in the world, but if you fail to listen to your customer, appear disinterested, or simply don't care, knowledge will not save you.

A customer is not interested in what you did last weekend or a product feature if that is not what they are looking for or solving a problem they have.

Knowledge is nothing unless you use it to answer the questions your client is asking.

Key Takeaways

- Customers will tell you more than they need to if you keep quiet and ask them open questions.
- Knowledge is a two-sided sword; one side can be used to confuse, overwhelm and create an atmosphere of superiority that will guarantee you do not get a sale; the other side can be the most powerful weapon you have when you add them together with listening and asking good questions.
- People buy People, so failing to make regular eye contact with your customer will inhibit your ability to create rapport and build trust.
- Show interest in what your customer is asking you and be genuine as it may come back to bite you; remember Julia Roberts character in "Pretty Woman" and how she was treated by one of the stores in Beverly Hills, Big Mistake, Big, Huge!
- Never assume what your customer needs; I always say sell them what they want, give them what they need.

Hunting Elephants with – Peter Plaut

Peter Plaut is consistently recognised as a leader in the industry. He has over three decades of experience as a salesman, banker, portfolio manager, and research analyst. Peter operates globally sourcing, researching, negotiating and structuring large capital markets deals. Peter has senior level relationships with some of the largest hedge funds, private equity funds, family offices, sovereign wealth funds, pension funds and banks in the US, Canada and Europe. Currently, Peter serves as an Executive Director of Wimmer Family Office and Wimmer Financial in London and separately has an advisory firm which has a JV with one of the world's largest Private Equity and Credit Opportunities funds. Peter is blessed with 6 children (3 sons and 3 daughters (including two sets of twins). An active philanthropist, Peter is active in many charitable organisations.

Hunting Elephants

Of course, I am not talking about hunting the largest land mammals on earth. I am talking about hunting for and closing massive deals anywhere from $150million to well over $1 billion.

Since the Covid-19 pandemic locked down the global economy, I have executed engagements of over $10 billion in real estate development financing across various assets classes including residential, mixed use, office, and hospitality. During the Great Financial Crisis of 2008, I was ranked as one of the Top Rising Stars of Hedge Funds. This track record acknowledges my ability to manage through crisis and create positive investment opportunities in all environments.

For me, success is determined by the individual. For some individuals, success is defined by financial achievement and for others personal achievement. For a Rock Star, success is fame and fortune. For an athlete, success is winning above all else. For someone with a critical illness, success is surviving. For a mom, success is raising her children to be happy. The meaning of success has changed for me over the years. For most of my childhood and adult life, success was measured by my monetary achievement alone. However, after going through some very difficult personal and professional challenges, I now define success in terms of family and health, while financial status has become less important. Indeed, I am a husband, son, and a dad to 3 amazing sons and 3 wonderful daughters. Nevertheless, the thrill of hunting elephants is my passion.

Being successful, no matter how you define it, requires hard work. There is no substitute for hard work and relentless determination. It has very little to do with luck! You make your own luck by working hard, putting the hours in, and setting yourself up for success. This means starting early (5am) and ending late at night (sometimes after midnight). Moreover, it requires planning and organising your day, week, month and year through setting attainable goals and adjusting as required because life is not linear.

For me, they key to success in sales is based on five principles:

1. Connections
2. Reputation
3. Authority
4. Passion
5. Follow up

Connections - If you want to be successful in sales you need to be continually growing your network, while taking great care of your existing clients. Prospecting is everything. I try to telephone call, video call and/or meet at last 2-3 prospective clients per week. That's an average of 10 per month, 120 per year. I rely on institutional investor relationships developed over the past 30 years, third party introducers, social media such as LinkedIn and referrals from existing clients. Most prospects will not become clients for various reasons, not least of which is the size of the deals that I am focused on – I only hunt Elephants! More importantly, time is money and there is only approximately 12 hours of workable hours in my day, thus if a potential client wants my focus on their deal there is an upfront engagement fee, a key milestone fee, and a large success fee that runs in the millions of dollars.

Reputation - Your reputation and integrity are all you have in both your professional and personal life. A good reputation will open a vast world of new opportunities and prospects. It starts by building your own brand. Your brand and your reputations are your most important asset and it's your identity.

Authority - Demonstrate immediately that you are the star athlete in your chosen field based on your knowledge, experience, and success in executing / closing deals.

Passion - If you are passionate about your career, you will be excited to show up every day. This excitement will flow thru to your client's perception of you and perception is everything in sales. Find a career that you are passionate about, excited to wake up to, and one that you love. It truly is the way in which you will never 'work' a day in your life.

Follow Up - I believe that a large part of my personal and profession success is because I am constantly following up with family, friends, colleagues, existing clients, past clients and potential clients. I regularly send emails, WhatsApp messages, make the effort to pick up the phone and call to check-in. All the while, I am constantly asking myself and them – How can I add value?

Chapter Six

Objections! Bah Humbug

For the most part, objections are just excuses, lies, and rarely the truth. Most people hide behind objections to avoid making a decision or hurting your feelings. We all know that people in sales have no feelings, just kidding, but in your clients' minds, they will do anything they can to not offend you, if they are uncomfortable deciding or have changed their minds.

If you are honest with yourself, you will admit that you will search for any reason you can, not to do something you don't want to do or are afraid of doing. It is a fact that people will do more to avoid pain than to experience pleasure.

You know that you love coming home and looking at a newly mowed lawn with a great garden and trimmed hedge. However, you hate the thought of doing all the things that need to be done to achieve that. Instead, you will look for as many excuses as you can not to open that back garden shed.

Your customers can be just the same; they know what you have offered is a great product or service but would rather wait than go through the pain of paying the money or asking the boss for approval.

The other side of the coin is worse; you have not qualified them. The result is you have not demonstrated that what you are offering meets their needs, which rests with you and your process.

All is not lost and, in most cases, can be overcome with a simple yes or no.

Peel the band-aid off

I remember telling myself that I was not too fond of cold calling businesses in person or walking up to a customer in a shop because they may yell at me or worse—what a load of rubbish that turned out to be. I mentioned previously, that salespeople are purported to have no feelings, and in many cases, that is how you need to act. I do not mean that we should ever tolerate rude or inappropriate behaviour, as what we tolerate is what we condone.

Instead, being stoic and showing no emotion to someone who is being discourtesy and inappropiate, can have the opposite effect on them and can earn you respect; in the end, if they do not change, is it worth it to have a customer that does not respect you, I think not.

Faced with a new job doing 'Hunting', which is canvassing around suburbs offering a product to a specific demographic, I soon learnt that I was dealing with highly stressed people who had little time for someone like me asking them to buy my product. I needed to change tact and fast.

I used rejection as fuel by deciding just to do it and see what happened, every rejection made me hungrier for the next sale, and when I succeeded, I rewarded myself. I soon realised that peeling the band aid off didn't hurt at all, all I was doing was inventing a reason not to do something.

In the end, rejection and objections just rolled off me like water off a duck's back, yes, I had tough days, but the same attitude gave me incredible days. The best thing you can do is just put your head down and keep going.

A word of advice though, if you find yourself having a particularly bad day and you just cannot get your mojo back, take a break, turn all the devices off and take a walk in a quiet place. People pick up on a lousy vibe and will automatically turn off on you.

I learnt this lesson later in life, today I have my favourite place to go to. I put on a 10 minute mediation or my favourite music and just chill. It is incredible what a reset will do for the mind and the presence you have.

Common objections

I can't afford it

This is the most obvious and common excuse people use. The majority of the time it simply is not the truth. It is just you have not demonstrated the value of the product or service. If you receive this objection on a regular basis, then your marketing is attracting the wrong client and needs to be reviewed.

I have to ask

Ah, this old fobb off, used by those not willing to decide or not able. If you have done your discovery correctly, you will know who you need to talk to enable a decision to be made. Dump timewasters and move to the decision-makers.

Ah, I don't know just yet

This is a indicator that something has occurred previously that you are not aware of. The client has been burnt and doesn't have faith or belief in making a decision due to their past experience. A great question to ask here is "Has something happened in the past that you had a bad experience with, and can I help in any way". Watch their body language and it will tell you what they are thinking.

If they say no, then ask, is there something you need clarified or expanded upon, that would address any concerns you may have? Again, observe how they react and don't pressure them in case you push them away and kill the deal.

I have to think about it

Just like the Titanic, your deal has struck the iceberg and is sinking fast. When someone tells you this, it is code for, I don't want your product or service, and rather than offend you, I will fobb you off.

In some cases, however, it can be saved when dealing with detail-driven people who like to make decisions in their own time.

A great way to see if you are treading water or sinking fast is to ask a simple question "Can you tell me what part of the offer or service you need to think about, and is there anything I can provide you with that will help you decide". The response will inform if you are able to rescue the deal.

The main reason it has gone south is you, that's right'; you; you have not sold the deal well enough for a decision to be made or at least provide a timeframe.

If we are completely honest, every professional salesperson will admit that they have done this and scuttled a great opportunity because they got excited and stopped listening or failed to meet the clients' expectations.

Be under no illusion this happens online, face to face, and with over-the-phone sales. No matter the medium, all the above tips can be applied to any form of commerce.

Side story

When I was a Sales Manager, I played a game with my team of "if you don't, I will". I would be with my team either sitting in a car or standing in the street. I would look up and see a prospective business and ask, have you been in there before, no would be the response, and

I would follow up with, well, why not, and are you going to go in. Watching the fear rise in their face, I would tell them if you are not going in, then I will, but I get the credit.

When I received an excuse, I would respond with, so on a Friday night out you see someone you want to buy a drink or dance with, do you have a problem approaching them? Well, what's the difference now.

They would go in with the directive of do not come back without an appointment, name, and number. Even better, I am happy to wait in case you get a chance to do a quick discovery discussion.

I have used the same tactic in retail situations and phone cold calling; some say it is brutal, I say it breeds a great belief that anything is possible. All you need to do is peel the band aid off.

Key Takeaways

- Objections are customers using an excuse not to hurt your feeling or get out of doing something uncomfortable.
- If you qualify your customer better, you will reduce the number of objections.
- Seek agreement along the way until you have met all their needs.
- Do not be afraid to ask what is stopping them from buying today if they flinch.
- Some people just do not decide on the spot, so it can be good to be patient but ask if there is any more information, they need to decide.
- Not all customers are worth the trouble.
- Salespeople do have feelings. We just choose not to show them all the time.

Making your own luck in Sales with - Rob Doorey

Short Biography

Rob has spent three decades as a radio presenter and Master of Ceremonies (MC). Working behind the microphone at more than a dozen radio stations and networked to many more. As an MC he has worked alongside Prime Ministers, big named music artists, sports stars and performed on some of the biggest stages in the Country. Rob is now a sought-after real estate auctioneer licensed in both NSW and Queensland, along the way he has held various managerial positions including State Sales Manager, Promotions Manager and is a very successful business owner.

> "Luck it ain't enough, got to make your own breaks"
> Bon Jovi - "It's my life"

Yep, I'm starting with a quote from Bon Jovi. With more than 30 years in commercial radio and admittedly a fan of the New Jersey rockers, it's as good a place as any to start. I feel very fortunate, very "lucky" in fact to have had the career I have. But that word luck...it's a funny one. While I do believe luck certainly plays a part, I think more over it's how you position yourself to be ready when "luck" comes along. I will come back to that later.

But first, looking back over my career (The rear-view is much easier, if not sometimes confronting than the future) I can recognise at least three important skills or qualities that I found helpful.

1. Determination and a willingness to be uncomfortable.
2. Communication. Probably the most important tool in any part of your life.
3. Back yourself.

Determination & a willingness to be uncomfortable

Wow, this is a big one. How many self-help books, training seminars and how to videos on this. How determined are you to achieve your goal? Is your goal just something that would be cool if it happened, but you're not willing to put too much effort into it. Many of the self-help books and sales strategies will talk about pain versus gain. As humans we have an unwillingness to take a step forward until the pain of doing so is less than what we feel right now. What a shame we must wait until our current situation is so dire before we are willing to take the leap.

Fortunately for me, when I started in radio, I was young, brash and although I would sweat profusely and be absolutely crapping myself, I loved the idea of being on radio more than how uncomfortable I felt. I still recall my first talk break on air. 1991 Coast Rock FM Gosford NSW and I could not get the words out quick enough. I am sure it was hard to decipher what I said. But in my mind, I was thinking "The quicker I get the words out, the quicker I can start the next song and have three and half minutes to get myself together before doing it all again!" But here's the thing, do it once, twice, a hundred times and it becomes less and less uncomfortable, almost second nature and we forget the "pain" that we went through the very first time. First steps - the worst thing to do is nothing...just do something.

Communication

My career began with communication and continues to be. Selling a product, selling yourself, selling a property - it's all communication.

On the radio I would be selling the music, a product by way of a live read or promotion and I would also be selling myself. Building a rapport with the audience, wanting them to warm to you and to feel good, informed or entertained listening to you. The same goes on stage as an MC or in front of buyers at an auction. In order to do this, you must have an interest in who they are. Who is my audience? What do they do? What are their likes? Dislikes? What inspires and interests them? Communication is a two-way street. So often we spend so much time talking about ourselves or what we are feeling and not enough listening or trying to understand our audience or our client. I love the saying "Why do we have two ears and only one mouth? Because we listen twice as much as we talk."

Back yourself

Ignore that little voice in the back of your mind telling you that either you're not good enough or you can't do it. Sometimes there are real voices in your life around you that may have a similar thing to say.

I remember when I told friends, family...anyone that would listen that I was going to be a radio announcer, very few backed me. Once I got my first gig, many would say "We knew you could do it" ...funny that.

When I started in radio in the early 90's, aspiring radio announcers would send out demos of their work on cassette along with a resume hoping to get a gig and be the next big thing. I must have sent hundreds of these over the years...and I was not the only one. Many would end up in a box beside the PD's (Program Directors) desk and never be heard. But if you got a bite - you were on it. I sent a demo to a PD at 4CA in Cairns (Hi Brad) and surprisingly he responded... even gave me some critique on how to improve, fantastic. I jumped straight back in the studio and gave it another go, sent the cassette off and waited for another reply.

Being impatient I suggested to my then girlfriend we should fly 3000 kilometres to Cairns for a holiday! She thought that was a great idea - little did she know it was more about me meeting this one PD who had even noticed I existed. My ruse was up on the first day when she wanted to go sunbaking and I wanted to go into town and "check out" the local radio station. No surprise that was the start of the end of that relationship.

That visit to "check out' the radio station eventually resulted in a job presenting the night-time countdown show only a few months later.

Which leads me back to "Luck" There's an old saying "Right place, right time." I have always believed "Be in the right place all the time, so you are there when the right time comes"

As an example, I got the job at 4CA, not because I was a good announcer, it was because I was the first name that came to mind when there was an on-air position available. I wasn't just a cassette in a box with a well written, if not embellished and sometimes exaggerated resume attached. I had also shown a willingness to listen to critique along with how keen I was. A 3000km trek to the top end will do that.

I think I may have gone over my word count (No surprise), but I hope there is something in here you can take away and assist you in whatever your big dreams and goals are. Let me finish with this, along with the aforementioned three skills or qualities, here are a few more to add to your toolbox. Have a strong work ethic, empathy, honesty, integrity and if the Covid epidemic has taught us anything, be ready to pivot. Those who adapt survive, those who don't won't. And lastly the three P's - Preparation, Practice, Plan. All the best.

Chapter Seven

Offer a Solution

A common saying from people who have had long-term success in the sales industry is:

"Solve their problem, Win the Sale"

It does not matter what you are selling unless there is a need or market for it then no matter the quality of the product or service, you are wasting your time if nobody wants to buy it. This chapter is all about Solution Selling and how by discovering what is driving your customer helps you become their best ally.

We all have a problem we need Fixing

People buy with emotion and justify with logic later, ask anyone who goes to their local shopping centre on the weekend and comes home with bags of stuff. We all hear them come in the door and say things like, "this was on sale" or "doesn't this look gorgeous" or even "I cannot wait to see the look on Jodie's face when I give this to her on her birthday" which happens to be six months away.

Tapping into that emotion when offering a product is gold and raises the opportunity of a successful sale above 50%. I do not mean that you should use that emotion to sell someone something they do not need or want because that person is easily manipulated. While that may get you a sale on the day, I am sure Karma, the vengeful elephant, will find you later, and it will be messy.

However, when you use the questioning techniques discussed earlier to dig deep into why the purchase is needed and frame the product to meet their needs, you can be on a roll.

Every person who goes into a takeaway food store is hungry or walks onto a car yard is looking for a car; it is up to you to find out why they need that car or how hungry they are. The same can be said in business sales.

A manager does not seek quotes for a tender or new office equipment unless there is a need. That is right; you can build a nexus between Problem and Need. An excellent point to remember is if you find the conversation going around in circles, do not be afraid to ask, "What is the most important thing you need me to solve for you today", or words to that effect.

By solving someone's problem, you create a need that you can fill. The client is more likely to tell the world how good you were and less likely to focus on price when the significant issue is solved.

They may have to justify later to their boss, sibling or partner why they spent what they did but deep down, they know it was the right decision.

Flipping

This section has nothing to do with cooking pancakes or selling homes; instead, it is a technique that can be used when you are stuck and going in circles, or you are just unsure why the customer is in front of you.

I have used this technique in many scenarios, and rarely has it failed me. Flipping is turning the tables around on your client and getting them to tell you why they asked you to their office or rang you on the phone. I find it best to use when a customer is not clear on what they need and how you can help them.

By simply asking the question, "what made you contact us today or similar", moves the customer to focus on what they are looking for and most times gets them to be open and tell you so much more about their problem or need.

In the best cases, it has resulted in the client justifying to me why they wanted to use our product and ended up selling my product to me without a single word because it provided them with the best solution.

You will find real estate agents use this a lot when they say, "so what is it you like about this house" within a minute or two, they will pick up if the person in front of them is interested in the listing or not and if they are keen listeners, they can pounce and offer them another property they have rather than lose a potential sale. This technique is also linked to Fishing Questions, i.e., open-ended questions that leave your client feeling obligated to answer.

Again, it is all about flipping the onus back on the customer rather than leaving it up to you to "SELL" and leave you open to not being successful.

Key Takeaways

When a new starter smells a sale coming, I know they will often get excited like a child in a candy store, jump straight past the questions, never seek their pain or problems, or ask what the client wants and jumps directly to the solution.

Boom, Boom, Crash and Burn rarely are we successful when we do that, and most salespeople who have been doing sales for any length of time, will admit we have all done this at one point in our careers.

Taking the time to discover what a client's pain, issue, motivation, or need is will always result in you providing the best solution for them.

- Solve their problem, Win the Sale.
- Every customer has a problem that needs fixing, and it is up to you to do that.
- Do not be afraid to ask what the problem is.
- Flipping the conversation will unearth the real issue.

A short case study

It always amazes me how much money is left on the table or sales missed by small businesses. So many times, an easy sale is right in front of you, and for some reason, people walk away.

I was told this story by a lady who has a two storey house with separate air conditioning units that looked after each level. Picture the middle of winter, and one of them decided to stop working.

Now this person had dealt with the original company that installed them for all her service needs for nearly ten years, so she arranged for the technician to come over and see what was wrong. The unit was worn out and in need of repair. The technician said that he would provide a quotation but, in his opinion, it was probably better to replace the unit with a new one and do the second unit when it also died.

A walk-up sale for a new unit in anyone's playbook. I am sorry to disappoint you, but five days later, a quote turned up to fix the existing unit, not the two promised, and no phone call from anyone from the showroom about buying a new replacement unit.

Another week past and an email was sent about the repair; no quote to compare for a new unit, so the homeowner decided to contact another company to come and quote for a new unit.

Quote request sent off; appointment date agreed to etc. but nothing scheduled in the salesperson calendar. Homeowner phoned back, apologies all round new time and date booked everything seemed hunky-dory.

Guess what no-one turned up for that appointment either.

The lesson here is that no matter how small or large your business is, if you do not have watertight processes in place on how you handle leads, you will miss sales.

Both companies lacked any actual process, and they will never know how many walk-up sales they have missed.

Chapter Eight

Stories Sell

I remember being at the pub at an early age, and you know the most popular guy at the table was the one that always had a story to tell, always making everyone feel excited, and it didn't matter if we believed him or not.

It was an excellent time to sit back and listen to someone else's story. In many ways, he is not that different from someone in sales. As a salesperson you are a storyteller.

His stories made him popular at the pub. In day-to-day sales, stories not only sell, but they also add more credibility, better than any factsheet, data, or salesperson trying to do their best to persuade someone.

There is nothing better when you are sitting listening to someone describe their biggest issue or challenge, and you know your product is what they need, but they are a hard nut to crack, and you can tell the perfect story.

There is an art to storytelling in sales, and when you get it right and tell a story that you believe in, there is nothing better. It also adds credibility to everything you are saying.

The most successful entrepreneurs all use stories. They didn't achieve their success without having a personal experience, something that has happened to a customer of theirs, or a real-time result that they use when needing to support a point.

Sharing these journeys is essential when it comes to selling and something every person in sales should master.

The foundations of a good Story

When we tell stories, we use them to sell a solution, the history of a product, or an idea of what might happen. All these lead to the same end, emotion. That's right, a good story creates emotion with your buyer, and that is what you want.

The better the storytelling, the better the sales results. This means your story needs to be as good or even better than the person telling it.

If you want to rock at storytelling, you need to include the following elements to ensure you have the best chance of success.

Own the Stage

How you enter a room, approach a customer, or walk out to do a presentation reflects on you, and people will judge you before you have even opened your mouth. Leave your bad day in the car and put your game face on. We are not all extroverts, however you need to be confident without being smug, this is crucial.

When you walk ensure your shoulders are back, head up, a big smile, firm eye contact, and acknowledge those in the room, this will set you up for success. If you need to, just before you enter, stop, breathe and remember you have got this.

Look around the room or shop as you walk in and see who is engaged, interested, or looking out the window, and you will know pretty much straight away what the vibe is. Retail is no different, just a smaller crowd but the same body language on show.

Main Character

A good book or film needs a lead character, which is no different from telling a story in sales. The lead can be a person, company, or group if it is tangible for your client to connect. This gives what you are telling instant credibility and allows your customer to buy in quickly as you build a connection between both.

The Story Behind the Story

The body or crux of what they were doing can also be called the setup. The client needs to know what they were trying to accomplish and how important it is to them. It does not matter if you are responding to your customers who want to travel around the country in a new 4WD or a guy buying his first suit. It is all the same. By linking your story to what your client wants to achieve, you get to show off your knowledge and build trust.

What's the Problem?

The issue or problem must match what your client is also experiencing so they can lean in and be part of the whole story. This works in two ways; it acknowledges that you have been paying attention to what they have been telling you and gives them comfort that they are not the only people who have the same issue.

So, when a customer hears that someone similar is trying to achieve the same thing as them and experiences the same challenges, you have them by the hook. All you need now is to reel them in with a great ending.

Winners are Grinners

The result or end of the story brings it all together and proves to them that what you are offering is what they need.

By bringing closure, you can deliver on what the future may look like when they buy this product, solve an important issue, or even feel part of something special.

A good story told correctly will give you better results than any clever one-liners or pretty graphs.

Now you have the script you need to perform the show, which can be fun.

How it all Fits

The Beginning

Like any good show, you need to set up the story, introduce your characters and what they do. It is important to show very early that your story relates to your client, and they become part of the journey.

The Middle

This is where we get to the crux of the whole tale, describe how the issue affected them or what they wanted to achieve and the pain it was causing.

The Ending

Time to wrap it all up by demonstrating the results that have been achieved and how they have been performing since.

Delivery

If you ask most people, they can tell you the "Bullshit Metre" is going off within a minute if they feel they are being lied to. When you deliver a story, be aware of the tone and pitch of your voice. What is your body language portraying, are you slumped in a chair or sitting upright and on the edge.

If you want someone to believe your story, you must believe it and be excited to tell it. What is the use of just blurting out words that you have remembered with no emotion? You will not get a sale and will more than likely never see this prospect again.

A customer will feed off your enthusiasm, and their emotions will rise with you as you show what is possible.

A story can be used to sell anything from an apartment in a city to a brand-new car or even a new dress to a woman who has a big event to attend.

When to tell a Story

Stories Sell that there is no question. All you need to do is to learn when to use them. I have found that there are a few times that it is best to go down this line.

Your customer could be a creative type that is not into details and is very chatty, or you are not getting buy-in from a customer, and they are starting to wander.

Both are effective in bringing back the balance of power to you.

Short and Sharp

It is agreed that most customers do not care about what you have done on the weekend or how your day is going unless they are also in sales and share your pain.

In saying that, sometimes a short sharp story and chance to put a smile on a person's face can break the ice and create instant rapport.

A smile is rarely not met with a smile in return. A laugh breeds curiosity, and an open question brings information.

You have approximately 30 seconds when someone first meets you to set the tone, so make good use of it. Do not be afraid to be funny or even better happy as people enjoy working with happy people. Paying someone a compliment on the office, clothes, day, whatever, if it is genuine, it will set the tone.

Yes, a short compliment is just the opening for a short story and brings the power back to you and will relax your customer.

If you share a story about yourself, make sure it is to the point with a quick setup, issue, result, and how it made you feel, all in 3 minutes or less.

Trust your gut on when to use this tactic and watch for a reaction from your customer.

Key Takeaways

- Having a good story that supports your product or service increases the success rate of your sales.
- The Story you tell must be honest and relevant.
- Energy equals results when it comes to delivery.
- You are as much the Story and what you tell.
- Do not be afraid to be funny or laugh as people like to do business with happy people.

"You are the opening chapter of your story"

The Art of Storytelling and Creating a Community with - Tara Solberg

Creative to her core and entrepreneurial in spirit, Tara Solberg is the founder and owner of both **Few and Far** *and* **Indigo Love**, *two halves of one thriving business based on the beautiful South Coast of New South Wales. Tara has built a multi-layered business comprising retail, wholesale and online offerings of one-of-a-kind treasures from around the globe and thoughtful homewares for which the brand is known.*

Along with her business, Tara is equally passionate about education and equipping fellow entrepreneurial women with the tools they need to thrive in business, which has led to the launch of TRADE WINS, *a collection of online courses and an accompanying podcast series.*

There is so much more to selling than exchanging goods or services for money. In fact, this should be the result of the engaging process that comes before this. I genuinely believe that the most important part of building a business and in turn achieving sales is not only creating a memorable brand, but creating an immersive and creative experience for your customer to enjoy and to *participate* in. No one wants to be sold to, but they will willingly participate if they are entertained and engaged. And if we are successful in our ability to invite them into our world, our own unique story, then sales will naturally follow. I'd go as far as to say that I can guarantee that the customer will not want to leave empty handed, and more importantly, they will want to visit again and again and invite others to do so too.

When Danny and I opened our first store in Huskisson NSW, we had a strong vision for the type of product we wanted to sell, the environment we wanted to create and more importantly, the experience we aimed to offer our customers. Fast forward to now, and we have carried this brand vision through everything we do, from product and branding, packaging, store fit outs, merchandising, marketing and our online experience. From the moment our customers are lured into our stores through the act of enticing their sensory curiosity, they are immediately transported to another time and place, another world, where they can get lost in time and enjoy the magical journey of discovery our stores have to offer.

In order to engage that sense of curiosity though, this journey of discovery needs to start before they enter the front door and is one of the most important elements of every touch point of our brand. What has brought them to visit you in the first place? How have you captured their attention?

This is where the art of storytelling or 'surprise and delight' is so important to playing a crucial role in customer acquisition. By thinking creatively and considering all touch points, be it the user experience when they sign up to our newsletter and receive a thoughtfully written welcome note or the moment, they receive a delivery of our product and take note of the considered details on how it comes packaged, you have the ability to create a customer for life. Invite them into your world and make them feel like they never want to leave, by enchanting them at every opportunity and strengthening the connection between the customer and your brand.

When it comes to designing and arranging any of our Few and Far stores, I always consider all of the senses – beautiful visuals, intoxicating aromas, relaxing music and luxurious textures. All of these elements become an extension of our brand story and work together to create a memorable experience. Our layered and plentiful merchandising displays portray confidence in the product we sell and present ideas or occasions for a product's use by inviting our customers into the story. The concept of 'upselling' works beautifully here, solely through the presentation and thought behind the merchandising layout, which removes the need for an awkward 'push' from a sales assistant, allowing customers to remain 'in the moment' and continue to enjoy their experience.

Our motto 'Bringing The World Home' illustrates the passion and dedication we have to creating spaces with meaning. We introduce pieces that have had a previous life or have their own stories to tell which can then be intricately woven throughout our own homes for the next chapter of its life. As important as these stories are though, they are lost without their storyteller. It is our responsibility to continue this story and to pass it on to our customers, who then share their appreciation of these unique pieces with their friends and family.

Ultimately though, the act of creating a *personal connection* with your customers will always have the biggest impact when it comes to driving sales and building brand loyalty. People affiliate with brands that reflect their own values, beliefs and aspirations. Through all of my 12 years of experience, I have learnt that taking the time to understand and nurture these relationships is key to achieving the successful outcomes you desire. Humans yearn for personal connection and the feeling that they belong to something bigger, a feeling of *community*. The customer and their experience should always come first, and when this happens, and we do our job well, we aren't having to *hustle* for sales or hard sell, but we will see a return on the generosity we have shared.

Summary

- The most important part of building a business and in turn achieving sales is not only creating a memorable brand, but creating an immersive and creative experience for your customer to enjoy and to *participate* in. Achieving the sale is the *end result* of this process.
- Focus on creating customer *engagement* through a *journey of discovery*.
- The art of storytelling or *'surprise and delight'* is so important to playing a crucial role in customer acquisition. Enchant them at every opportunity which in turn will strengthen the connection between the customer and your brand.
- Consider appealing to the senses for a *memorable* experience
- Build the *feeling of community* and nurture these relationships through *personal connection* based on your values, beliefs and aspirations. Nobody wants to be sold to.

Chapter Nine

Tongue Tied

The words we use are more powerful than any advertisement, pretty gift wrap, or fantastic price. They can get us into trouble or bring us pleasure. In sales, they are one of the most powerful tools you can have and should be nurtured, practiced, and chosen wisely.

This chapter will look at some tips to ensure we do not get tongue tied by what we say and learn to control what words we use.

> *Whatever words we utter should be chosen with care; people will hear them and be influenced by them for good or ill.*
>
> **Buddha**

Words, Words, Words

Words will trap us every time; what we want to say, what we say and what we try to say can get us all into trouble. When we get excited, we seem to join all our words together or blurt them out without engaging our brains. This leads us into alleyways that we do not want to enter and sometimes to dead ends with no way out.

When you find yourself getting excited or starting to jabber, there is a simple tool everyone can use and one that the best presenters do without even thinking.

I call it "The power of the pause" that's correct pausing before you answer even when you know what you are saying is 100% accurate is more powerful than anything else.

Try it next time you are in discussion with opposing views, without realising it the power of the moment will be with you.

Have you ever been in a discussion or been asked a question from a client that you either do not understand or cannot remember what the answer is? Well, there is a way that you can buy time and get out of trouble.

A former high-ranking politician in Australia gave me this advice about handling tricky questions, especially from journalists. When asked a question you are not sure of, repeat it back to them in a slower beat; this will give your mind time to catch up, a chance to remember the answer, and it gives the person asking the question the feeling that you are genuinely paying attention to what they are saying.

Words create Emotion

The great authors of all time use words to create a picture of an event and have the power to take you to places that you have never been, to move you through time or to give your insides a tingle of excitement or even horror.

It is no different when it comes to selling, a good salesperson knows the words that will instil a reaction in their client or customer. It is possible to make even the most boring product or subject sound exciting and inviting.

You can also use words to create in your customer's mind the feeling of what might happen if they make that purchase, and as we know, people buy with emotion and justify with logic later.

Listen closely to the advertisements on radio or TV, you can distinguish the keywords or comments they use to entice you to buy that product. "Clean, sparkling dishes," "crystal clear screen," "safe, comfortable ride".

Of course, you cannot physically see what they are talking about in the radio advertisement, but you immediately know what they are conveying.

Mirror, Mirror

Another great tool used by those who negotiate, and close more significant deals is the technique of Mirror, Mirror which has nothing to do with how you look.

This technique is when you listen intently to what your customer is saying and use their words back when pitching and closing. When used correctly, it is compelling and leaves your client nowhere to go as they cannot disagree with their own words.

Keep Control

Sometimes, when we are speaking, our tongues move quicker than our minds, and our mouths become dry under pressure. It is not uncommon and is easily fixed.

It is crucial to manage our energy and excitement when we are keen for a sale or even worse, when a presentation is going south. We have all done it, and I have been guilty myself of brain freeze at the most inappropriate time.

We discussed the power of the pause earlier in the chapter, which I believe is one of the most powerful tools you can use to reset a conversation, except when your body decides to play tricks with you.

Before

When I was younger, I used to run like a bull at a gate into meetings and pitches, only to be knocked out of the park in the first few minutes. It took me a while and some mentoring before I found a way to control my emotions and ensure I did not get frazzled.

Now, I like to have a coffee and go to a quiet place before any crucial meeting; it allows me to centre my thoughts and be comfortable with all the information I need to succeed. You can do the same in retail or call centres when you have had a demanding customer, and the next one is waiting. Taking a 2 minute time out will make all the difference.

When I am visiting an office or site for the first time, I like to do a drive past a day earlier, if possible, so I know where I am going. I also like to arrive 15 minutes early, so I am not rushing, because when we do it always results in a less than acceptable performance.

During

If you are in an office situation, never sit with your back to the door; one it is bad feng shui and two you can't see who is walking in.

Ensure you have set an agenda before arriving and repeat it at the start of the meeting to reduce the likelihood of surprises.

Remember to breathe; it sounds silly, I know, but when people get excited on stage or in a presentation quite often, they forget, and suddenly, they have to concentrate on catching their breath rather than the conversation in front of them.

Dry mouth or lockjaw can come on very quickly, especially if you are getting hammered by someone across the desk or counter; two easy fixes for this, take a sip of water if available and pause, or second, imagine you are swallowing a giant orange. Both will return the inside of your mouth to normal.

Deflect, deflect, deflect is a term used by politicians and lawyers when they do not like the question. I am a fan of always being upfront and honest, but there will be times when your brain refuses to engage, so a couple of deflecting questions back to the customer will allow you to catch up.

Leaning forward will show that you are interested, even if you are not, and leaning back indicates you are comfortable with the conversation. Use these two wisely as the people in front of you will read them and assume accordingly.

After

How you leave or finish a meeting is just as important as how you start. Your words or gestures as you finish up, can scuttle a deal very quickly. I remember being in one of my first meetings as a very inexperienced salesperson and watched as my boss did everything right from what I could see.

The customer was giving us great feedback, and I thought we had the deal done. Wrong, my boss had assumed the same and got very relaxed with his words and posture, which conveyed to our customer that he had it in the bag.

Assuming you have the deal before you close is fatal and something I found out later when I went back to visit. The customer told me that they had gone with a different supplier because of the "in their eyes" arrogant behaviour of my boss. Words and actions mean other things in different cultures, and my boss had insulted them without even knowing it at the time.

Always check before finishing a meeting or closing that everything has been covered and how your client would like to proceed. This makes them feel comfortable and using words that give them a feeling of value and respect ensures you have a better chance of success.

Footnote: I did continue to call on this customer regularly and won them over about a year later, and by their request, my boss was never allowed back.

Buzz Words

It can be very easy to assume the person we are speaking with knows all about the product we are selling, even worse trying to impress them with very product specific vocabulary only proves that you are a try hard.

The term, keep it simple, is so true it is scary. Customers won't let you know they have no knowledge as a rule because they think it puts them in a vulnerable position.

Some interesting customers will fake not knowing anything just to test your knowledge, which can be frustrating.

I recommend keeping the conversation to uncomplicated words as a rule until your customer has spoken and you can react to what language they are using. Buzz words can put a client off unless you know for sure they are aware and use the same terminology.

If in doubt ask your client if they require further clarification, this will open them up and you can proceed from there.

> ### *Key Takeaways*
> - Choose your words carefully.
> - Words have different meanings to different people.
> - When in doubt, pause, count to 3, then respond.
> - The opening and closing of a meeting are equally important.
> - Avoid buzz words.

Blah! Blah! Blah!

This is how you sound when you don't engage your brain before speaking.

Chapter Ten

The Power of Social Media

Whether we like social media or not, you cannot deny that it now plays an integral part in the sales process. I guarantee you that if you have a new product or business, before you have put the phone down or leave the building, somebody has searched your name on the internet.

Social proof of existence and people's ratings can make or break you; zero presence on Facebook, Instagram, LinkedIn, or even Tik Tok will impact if they move forward with you and is an integral piece of the jigsaw of getting a sale over the line.

The same can be said of retail/destination businesses where social media should be used as part of your sales funnel to encourage business your way.

I have often met a new customer with a complex supply issue and later noticed that someone from their company had checked my LinkedIn profile.

You do not have to be an expert in all social media platforms and do not need to be on everyone, but by creating a presence and using it to sell without selling can deliver huge rewards.

Facebook

Whatever you personally think of Facebook, you cannot question that it is the number one social media platform. I recommend that you secure your personal profile to friends only and have a "page" or Business profile.

When it comes to Facebook and sales, it can be used in two different ways. First, you can use it as your personal profile to promote your business profile, which is fine if everyone who befriends you on your profile knows that it is purely for business and not for personal use.

Many people will have two profiles: their business profile where they talk about everything to do with their business, and then a private profile that isn't open to the public, and only their friends can see.

The second one, is to have a business Facebook to promote your business, again it is essential you link it through to your YouTube for all your videos that you put up and automatically post back and forth on your Instagram. The important thing, no matter what you're doing or what your posting, is that you're providing value; in other words, you're not just posting for the sake of posting. Ensure your content value adds.

The goal of all your posts should be to encourage engagement; in other words, ask a question, put up an exciting photo and get people to engage with you so you can interact with them.

Facebook does limit the reach of your posts, they do encourage you to use ads, and of course, that's their way of increasing their profit. Facebook allows you to target your audience by filtering the demographic, age group etc. of who will see your advertisement so you're not wasting your money.

In my opinion Facebook, is more effective when you develop a campaign involving YouTube, Instagram, and any other social media platform that you consider your target audience will be on. Take the time to utilise services like "Canva" to create professional looking ads and posts that have a modest cost. This will increase the number of people who are interacting with you, and every campaign should link back to your website.

Today websites are the last or second last point of contact, and social media platforms are the funnel that is used to drive people to the business website or landing page.

I encourage everyone to follow a few basic rules when utilising Facebook; post regularly, provide value, make your posts engaging, and always with a picture. This will ensure that you're going to have the most interaction with your customers. Don't be afraid to check out what your opposition or other people within your company are posting on Facebook or social media. If they're doing something that you're not and it's working for them, why not copy them.

If you are unsure, just start with a Facebook page, create some advertisements with a small budget and see what feedback you get.

Instagram

Instagram is a personal favourite of mine, if your product or service is mainly visual, fun, or tells a story through pictures. Being also part of the Facebook family, it is easy to link them, so when you post on one, it will post on the other; you get two for one deal.

Again, you do not need to be an expert to use this platform, just the ability to write a short story and add an interesting or captivating picture.

The most important point you need to remember, is that Instagram is a visual medium, your product or service must suit the visual landscape. I always say people buy people and people also buy with their eyes. It is like when you're walking down the street, and something catches your eye in a store window, you may not buy it, but you will investigate it further. The same thing occurs on Instagram.

When you start your Instagram account look at what your competitors are doing that are gaining lots of likes and interactions. Ask yourself, what would I like to see on Instragram if I was the customer. Would it be a new employee's picture, details of a new product or a story about what's happening behind the scenes at the office or shop.

There are a couple of rules you should never forget when using Instagram, post regularly at least four times a week around the same time, ensure that your posts are linked back to your Facebook page or site, make sure that all your contact details are in your bio and use hashtags to attract extra followers.

If you are a cake maker and you're taking a photo of a fantastic cake you just made, put a hashtag along the line of #cakemaker #icing #baking.

Instagram now has a groovy feature where you can upload short videos; you can record them directly under the storyline above or put it as a post. Remember these videos are designed to be a couple of minutes long at most to grab your client or your follower's attention, be fun and invite your followers to be part of your story.

Another great way to increase your followers is to comment on other people's posts. When you do this, people look at who you are, and quite often, they'll start following you, which then increases your marketing reach and builds what we call social proof.

Remember, when you keep Instagram entertaining, people will keep following you; not everything has to be serious but remember everything must be in line with your branding and who you are.

LinkedIn

This has been called Facebook for serious people and business; either way, it operates very differently from the other mediums and should be treated that way.

More suited to personal business profiles with links back to your website, you can post technical and business articles to create standing as it is used by professionals when recruiting or deciding if a person, they are dealing with is the real deal.

In my opinion, it is the best place to share your opinions on current issues, opportunities, and new products that have a direct business value.

The advantage of LinkedIn is that it is the social media version of business networking. It's up to you to make the most of it. One of the important things about LinkedIn is you must remember it is the business version of Facebook, so it's not about pretty pictures of a cat, it is purely for business and building your network.

LinkedIn will help you set up your profile and your business profile correctly, and the best part is every time someone views your profile, it sends you a notification, so you know who's looking to see what you're doing.

Your competitors also monitor LinkedIn, so don't be fooled into putting up sensitive or proprietary information because they will grab it and use it, once goes on the world wide web, it's public knowledge.

YouTube

No not for me, it's only video's or I don't know how it works, YouTube that's just for young ones. These are generally comments of people who don't understand the power of YouTube, haven't watched it, or examined where it fits into the marketing area of sales and social media for their business.

When used correctly, YouTube can be a a powerful social media and advertising tool that costs you very little, and every business can use it.

The first thing anyone should do is take the time to see if their competitors are on YouTube, are there videos on YouTube that talk about your product. Why not type into YouTube a question about the product or service you supply and see what comes up. You will be able to see if there is a market or need and if anyone else is doing what you are doing.

The power of YouTube is that when you upload a monthly video, it is there permanently and can be linked back to your website.

Some key points to remember is that YouTube isn't for every business, but if you have a product that's either technical, is unique, or is visual, then you can make it work for you.

It's a great place to put up how-to videos or answer question videos, as I call them. An example is if you supply paint, create a video about how to paint a bedroom; it's not about selling, it's about giving people the information they need to do it. By doing this you've got your brand there, you place the links in the show notes, and suddenly, your company becomes the expert in how to paint a bedroom.

If you are super confident then try a question-and-answer session using YouTube live.

Tick Tok and Twitter

I believe the jury is still out on Tik Tok and Twitter in being a valuable sales tool due to the lack of specific market penetration when it comes to the sales industry. Both mediums are excellent in what they do and the market that they attract, but when it comes to sales, I'm not convinced both give you the penetration required to make them valuable.

Tik Tok is probably the one that's growing the quickest as it is a short-form video sharing platform from 30 seconds up to three minutes. It is excellent to target the youth market and react quickly to influencer-style videos. It may be the avenue for your product, but you will need to be precise when it comes to your video and have your message out there promptly.

Do your research, and if your demographic is watching, then go for it, I would never rule it out.

Twitter is more social commentary, news and made for quick dissemination of information rather than a business tool for sales. Twitter users can find themselves getting harased, chastened, or, as I call it, trolled by people who don't know their product and don't like what you stand for from a business point of view.

Although, it is an excellent platform for finding out the latest news, I don't think it is something that you really should use as a sales tool. I would be cautious of making comments that could come back to you bite you. In today's environment, emphasis is placed on who you are and what you stand for. It is very easy for a comment to be taken out of context, which could do irreversible damage to your brand, business and bottom line.

Key Takeaways

The key points to remember from this chapter are

- Research which social media platform your customers are using.
- Post regularly across the platforms that work for you.
- Keep your posts engaging and always provide value.
- Remember people buy people, if they don't like what you're posting, they won't buy your product regardless of how good it is.
- Start now.

Chapter Eleven

The Most Important Word in Sales, NO!

When I first started in sales, I was continually told that "the customer is always right" or "you never say no to a customer, just find a way".

Both statements are correct and incorrect, depending on the context. For example, in an order room, phone are constantly ringing, production is struggling to fill supply, customer complaints are escalating due to unsatisfactory levels of service and sales staff are at a breaking point due to the environment they are working in.

Conflicting strategies within a business can result in customers threatening to leave. This is a real scenario I was presented with by a client who was working within such an environment, and his senior's response to fix it, was, do not say no to a customer. After I picked myself off the floor and took a breath, I understood that while the intent was genuine, the result could be disastrous.

Every time staff said yes after this directive, another straw was added to the camel's back until one day it broke. Turnover and retention of order room staff was difficult, delivery drivers started to take sick leave, and team morale was at an all-time low.

Yes, we fixed it, it took time, energy, a change of attitude and words. The sales and the bottom line increased, retention of staff improved, and the company employed a new senior manager to run the order room.

What happens when you do not say "No" to a customer

Sales are also about who has the power in a negotiation and being subservient to customers is never the answer for good business. One sales process that you should definitely follow is to always manage your "customers' expectations". Being able to say no to a client is one of the most important skills you can have and saying no can be communicated in various ways. But before we delve into that, let look at what happens when we do not manage your customer's expectations.

Customers will always ask for more until there is no more to give, much like a child, and can behave like one when told no. Just like a child, if you always say yes to their request, they begin to behave badly with unreasonable demands, which can place strains on the business.

Visualise an exceptionally busy warehouse, with efficient systems that service customers quickly. The economy is slowing, effecting sales, the order room manager (noticed I said manager, not leader) decides the best way to fix the decline in sales, is to never say no to a customer, take every order and pass on to dispatch to fix. Great in theory but lousy in practice.

While one-off requests, should always be treated that way, the flow-on effect is much worse than any downturn in sales when you do this.

Once the workflow of any business is constantly interrupted with unrealistic requests, then the whole company is affected, and service levels drop.

Not saying no is very different from not saying yes. It is easy to say yes to every request, hope for the best, and pray that the camel's back does not break.

Every time a business and you don't say no, in the correct manner. Is one step closer to a meltdown for your staff and processes, which could effect revenue, turnover and lost customers.

Saying "No" can mean Yes!

The most important thing to remember when saying no to a customer is that two things occur.

1. The power shifts back to you when done correctly.
2. The opportunity for you to look like a star in their eyes is enormous.

Customers can be funny beasts. They can pretend to be your friend one minute, and the next, they are down the road at your opposition. Firstly, they usually only leave when they have been made an offer they cannot refuse, or you have not managed their expectations correctly. Setting boundaries (terms and conditions) around what you can and cannot do early on is vital when dealing with long-term clients. It is also essential when looking after short-term single sale transactions.

A great example:

Customer:

Can I have a large bag of fried chicken, please?

You:

No problem, that will be $12.50 and will be ready in 15 minutes

Customer:

I am in a hurry can you do it in 5 minutes

You:

I would love to, but all of our chicken is cooked fresh to order, so that we keep it to a high quality.

Managers will, however, always push the envelope compared to leaders. Managers will ask you to speed up the process and don't worry about quality. Leaders, however, will look at this as an opportunity to explore if the chicken can be cooked quicker using a different process without jeopardising quality or taste.

In business everyone is in sales and at times when we have to say no, we must ensure we do it in a way that customer is managed, needs are met if possible and the business not impacted. Offering an alternative to their request will show that you are trying to assist them rather than just saying a hard no, being in a corner, and having no way out.

Sometimes, we need to say no, only because by saying yes, we know we will never meet the client's needs, and if it goes wrong, you will lose them as a customer, they will tell others how you under delivered and bad news travels. The alternative is to be honest and advise that you cannot fulfill their request at this time, you have explored every avenue, and it is not possible. If you are honest about a situation, they will respect you for it even if they are disappointed in the short term.

I have experienced being yelled at by customers when I have said no. I have explained why I was not able to assist them, then to have them call me two weeks later to say thank you.

The difference was the person in the role before me, consistently said yes, and was not honest with what they could and could not deliver. When I commenced in the role, I was honest and upfront with all my clients, after a while, they knew what I was like, and we learnt to work together, so I never had to say no again.

> ### *Key Takeaways*
> - Never be afraid to say No.
> - Saying Yes, all the time can lead to more pain later.
> - Explore all options and offer them.
> - Continually manage your customers' expectations.
> - Leaders look for opportunities, and Managers look for a process.

"I cannot do what you are asking, but we can do this"

Saying "No" by saying Yes!

Chapter Twelve

Practice

Whoever thought that you would need or should practice selling methods but, just like any skills, you need to be comfortable in what you are doing. In coaching, this is referred to as unconscious competence, that is, when you do something without thinking, like tying your shoelaces.

Did you honestly think that a Tony Robbins, Michael Jordan, Ash Barty or Simon Sinek ever achieved anything without practise? The best in every genre of business and sport have committed themselves to hours of honing their skills so when the time came to perform, they were ready.

A salesperson should be no different.

> *"Life is 10% what happens to you and 90% how you respond to it"*
>
> **Fredrik Eklund**
> **Million Dollar Listing New York**

Practice makes Perfect

This is about getting it right or as close to right as possible. We all have heard about the basketball players who shoot thousands of hoops, so when they get to game day, they have a higher percentage of shots in the basket, than this is no different.

Before you practice, you must know your product. It does not matter if it is women's clothing, a welder, or motorbike; no well-rehearsed line or skill will get you that sale if your knowledge isn't up to par.

Take the time to be informed about all the details of the product or service you have, so you come across as confident and an expert when you are speaking to your customer.

Write down every question you anticipate that you will be asked, no matter how trivial, and write down the answers. I guarantee this will save you so many times it will scare you. With highly specialised products, it will become your cheat sheet and saviour.

Next, get a work buddy or friend to throw the questions at you, rapid-fire to see how you go. Even ask them to find ones you have not written down. Do this until you no longer need to refer to the sheet or make any errors.

A good tip here is to practice your eye contact, as people will observe your face, and any glimpse that may give the impression that you do not know your product could scuttle the sale.

If you are selling over the phone, try smiling while you are talking. This might sound odd but it works as people have a way of knowing if you are happy, confident, or reading from a script just by listening to the tone and pace of your voice.

Competition breeds Success

If you want to see an actual blood sport, put two salespeople against each other from the same company and ask them to present, sales professionals can smell blood, and the chance to beat one of their own is something they cannot resist.

You can use it to your advantage by writing out different sales scenarios and having your colleague pretend to be the client and grill you, you can then take turns with each other. While it could place you in an uncomfortable position, as you do not know what questions are coming your way, it will ensure you get great at focusing.

Another great role play is to have multiple sales situations, each of you pick one and present in front of colleagues, not from your department, who then provide feedback. Remember, you do not want people who will tell you what you want to hear; a customer certainly will not; instead, you want honest, constructive feedback.

It is only during these uncomfortable sessions that you will truly grow and evolve. If all else fails, have some relatives test you on your knowledge; they will indeed do you no favours and most likely end up being your biggest fan.

Short Case Study

At a sales conference, a facilitator had separated the sales team and managers. The sales team were discussing the different strategies of sales and the styles of customers. The managers were doing a similar task but with a negotiation focus as they looked after contracts etc.

The facilitator decided to change the dynamic and had the teams change roles. Sales would now be the managers, and vice versa. They were given the same scenario but from a different perspective and asked to negotiate an outcome.

The goal was to put both teams in a situation that made them uncomfortable where they had to use all their skills to get a result. What happened was nothing short of a real beating of the managers by the sales team.

The managers knew the technical side of the products and were used to coming from an area of power as they were normally the ones buying the product. The sales team had practiced listening, responding, knowing the product, and being able to read body language, as soon as the managers showed the smallest hesitancy in their responses, they went in for the kill and started to shut them down.

Before the sales team could have the managers in the corner cowering, the facilitator called a halt.

After a short break where the managers needed to cool down as they thought they had been made to look foolish. Both sides started to unpack how they had performed in the scenario.

The managers realised that while they had all the technical knowledge and were used to being in charge, they had never learned the art of empathy and had never prepared or practiced answering questions without notice. They acknowledged that this was their error and something they needed to work on.

The sales team thought they had done everything correctly; yes, they might have come away with a fantastic deal but, they potentially set themselves up for a significant loss later by not acknowledging when it is time to back off and play the long game. They all agreed that the skills the sales team practices every month at their meetings were so ingrained in their methodology that it had made them a very talented team and set a high benchmark for everyone else.

Key Takeaways

- Sales is no different to any skill, practice makes you better.
- Benchmark yourself against those who are better than you.
- Identify your weak spots and work on them.

Chapter Thirteen

Be your best self

The only way you can perform in any job, especially sales, is to look after yourself. Be healthy in mind and body, and the rest will look after itself.

I have not always done this, and my results when I have not looked after myself reflected it, so remember to always be true to yourself and do not make excuses.

This chapter will take you through some of the experiences and learnings that have shaped what I believe, and my wish is that you also learn to be better than you were last week.

> *"The goal is not to be better than the other man, but your previous self"*
>
> **The Dalai Lama**

Look in the Mirror

Take the time to work out who you are and what you believe in. There will be times when you do not win or get the sale, and it is easy to blame others, but the only actual competition to you is you.

Know what you are good at, use it to your advantage, know what you need to improve, and make it happen. Never be afraid just to be you. If you try to be someone you are not, customers will pick that up, and if someone is not willing to accept who you are, then ask are they worth it.

I follow a football team with more losses than wins, and all my customers know who I follow. It does not bother me in the slightest while others hide when their team loses.

I am known for being true to my word, and a handshake is your bond; at the same time, I have walked away from customers whose word is not worth anything—especially those who lie. Remember, your integrity is never for sale and is the most priceless commodity you own.

Opinions are just that Opinions

Opinions are just as easy to source as excuses, but in the end, they are just an opinion. It does not matter what anyone else thinks of you. I used to take things very personally and craved approval from others as validation that I was a good person. When I realised that the only person, I needed to get approval from was myself, things changed.

Listen to what others say, respect their right to have an opinion, take on board what is relevant, but in the end, you are the one that needs to be true to you.

You must always sleep at night being happy with your efforts and commit to being even better tomorrow.

Know what tickles your Fancy

Your purpose in life fuels much of what we do. Maslow's Hierarchy of Needs states that all humans crave or need to survive. Physiological (food and clothing), safety (job security), love and belonging needs (friendship), esteem, and self-actualisation.

The first four needs drop off as we meet them, however the last one of self-actualisation throws a curveball in that as we start to achieve, our motivation increases.

A truly motivated salesperson knows what gets them excited and performing well. It is not money as that is purely the result of what we do. Think hard about what puts that smile on your face. Is it the thrill of the chase for new clients, securing a significant contract, or even seeing a customer smile when they are happy with the purchase they have made?

Whatever it is, everyone is different but, in the end, it always comes back to a feeling of happiness.

Failure is my Oxygen

I will tell you something I never told myself when I was growing up. Failure is good; it drives you and gives you the boost you need to rock. When I was young, I was the opposite, never wrong and always looking for an excuse to get out of trouble.

It took many years of lost opportunities to realise that I was wrong sometimes and made mistakes that I needed to accept and take responsibility for.

Navy Seals are a great example of this as they work as one team; when they win, the whole group wins, when they lose, the entire team loses, and they take responsibility for their actions as a whole and look for ways to ensure they improve next time.

We all need to embrace our failures, even celebrate them as a way of letting go of a bad situation, and then use that same emotion as fuel that fires us up to get back up and be successful.

Exercise and Sleep

These two should be a no-brainer but are often the first to be forgotten when we get busy or have the opportunity for a good night out.

I know too many times I have turned up to work on a weekend, and well, let's say I could have done with a few more hours of sleep than I thought I got. How did I go? ok, commitment on the day 10/10, performance on the day 3/10. Not much more really to say here but find the optimum amount of sleep you need and get it.

Exercise can be more than just keeping physically fit; it is also a great way to escape and think. I believe any physical activity we do at any time is good, and you are the only one that should decide what's best but do something. I was told by a Senior Member of Parliament that when he needed to make a tough decision and required a clear mind, he would use a run to relax his brain and give him focus.

I recommend finding an activity you enjoy doing and using it the same way. I like to walk; others box or lift weights, do what brings you clarity and focus.

You are who you Hang around and Hold on To

Negative Nellies are what I call them timewasters and tie-me-downs, which all need to be dealt with. A common saying in coaching is that you are the sum off the five people you hang out with, so true, so don't hang out with people who do not share your passion or celebrate your success.

Negative people will always look for any way to minimise your success and growth, they are the black holes of the business world. They will suck the life out of anyone they meet because they do not understand the gravity of what you are doing, are jealous of what you have achieved and are just too bloody lazy to do the hard work that you have.

If a work colleague or friend cannot acknowledge and celebrate your success, no matter how big or small, I am sorry but dump them. They will be like a giant anchor around you, holding you back and sending self-doubt thoughts into your mind. Every season we edit our wardrobes, isn't it time we also did this with who we allow in our lives both personally and professionally.

The same thing can be said about a bad experience from the past, do you hold onto a hot plate till it burns you, or do you put it down. So why the hell do you hold on to old experiences that only serves to eat away at your confidence. Drop it like a hot plate and move on.

The same can be said of time-wasting customers who never seem to make decisions or are vague about what they want. They might be the nicest people, but they are holding you back from real customers unless they can decide what they want. Break up with them gently and inform them that you will be there, when they are ready.

Success attracts success, so be ready for new connections.

Key Takeaways

Being in sales is no different to be an athlete, to win you must be healthy in mind and body.

- Be true to yourself.
- Opinions do not matter.
- Let failure fire you.
- Keep healthy if you want to win.
- Let bad experiences go.
- Who you hang out with, you become.

Mastering your stage with - Adam Thompson

Adam Thompson

Adam Thompson is an Australian singer/songwriter, entertainer, philanthropist and entrepreneur. Widely acknowledged as one of the country's greatest entertainers, he is best known as the iconic front man of Australian rock band Chocolate Starfish, renowned for his powerful performances and electric stage presence.

On his entrepreneurial stage, Adam flourishes as the founder and creator of MusoMagic, a group song writing platform that engages people of all ages and backgrounds in creative exploration and expression. From school classrooms, remote Indigenous communities, Indian shelter homes to large-scale corporate events, MusoMagic has evolved under Adam's guidance to influence thousands of people all over the world.

Mastering Your Stage

'All the world's a stage, and all the men and women merely players.'

This famous phrase written by William Shakespeare compares the world to a stage and life to a play. While I concur, I challenge his use of the word 'merely' here. We are not so simple. Most of us never reach the extent of our full potential. Not because we aren't capable, but rather to be the best and to be ready when the opportunity comes, it requires daily practice and experiential learning, by extending our stage far beyond the boundaries of conventionality.

As an entertainer, I have strutted many hundreds of stages over my career. But it's what I do beyond the literal stage that plays a more crucial role in my success as an artist. By extending my stage, I am open to endless possibilities.

Essentially your stage is wherever your energy is – wherever YOU are.

Mastering this requires focus on these three things: performance, connection, and extension.

Performance

In sales we think of selling ourselves, or our brand, to compete against our competitors to gain market share. But what if we flipped the standard concept and realized our power was not in convincing another of our worth, but in simply being the best version of ourselves?

In our authenticity, we are 'selling' without trying to sell.

It is natural to want to compartmentalize ourselves into the face we show at work, at home, at play, to symbolize how much of ourselves we reveal in certain circumstances. While I understand there are variable levels of authenticity and vulnerability we are prepared to offer in each circumstance, I find that the thread of authenticity is often non-existent because the faces of these different personas are so different it is almost Jekyll and Hyde in in nature. There is no bedrock on which to build our foundation and we are responsive without substance in a never-ending cycle of trying to accommodate.

When we are so busy swapping and changing hats the essence of our individual strengths is diluted to mediocrity. Not only is it mentally exhausting, it's easy to see through and to be felt by others. How often have you been in a meeting where someone is delivering their spiel, but you don't believe that they believe it themselves? This occurs when there is a lack of authentic conviction, and the performer doesn't feel it. In comparing this to my experiences, I will always connect with an average singer performing something they truly feel and believe in, over technical brilliance delivered without connection. When our daily performance is grounded by consistently living your truth it is indelibly easier to shine.

Connection

These days, getting people to focus long enough to hear your message is a challenge. In some humans, however, there is a magnetism that pulls you towards them, compelling you to pay attention even before they say much at all. More often than not the power of this draw lies in one's risk in being vulnerable. Similarly, in my world of rock and roll, it's this vulnerable risk that not only captivates audiences and garners fans but leads the artist to greater potential. Essentially it is awareness of self and others in the moment. Being 'right here, right now' in the moment provides cues and clues to energetic flow that you can build upon. As an entertainer it is this unspoken connectivity between audience and performer that they are both on a journey together. If either one is detached from the experience, the energetic flow is diminished and clunky. If it's driven by the performer and both are in sync, magic moments flow almost to the point of feeling supernatural. As the performer, you guide this connection by opening yourself to your audience – whether it's an audience of one or one thousand.

Extension

Every day we have the potential to inspire or 'sell to' a new audience. Even someone you see regularly has the capacity to see your performance through fresh eyes if your delivery varies from what they expect.

We are evolutionary by nature and there is always opportunity to learn new skills in selling who you are or what you are selling. Some of us have brilliant techniques that worked perfectly five years ago, but today they might seem dated or predictable. By extending our stage literally and metaphorically, we open up to experimenting with other ways to deliver 'the goods'.

Throughout my 30 years of performing, I have pushed the boundaries of my stages, leaping off and creating new ones - perching myself on a giant speaker, climbing a light tower or jumping on top of a bar and parading it like a catwalk, changing where the audience views me and taking them on a journey with me.

I also push the boundaries of dress, as it's an important part of my stage presence. A bit of bling, a leather kilt, swinging fringe…not everything has met with unanimous praise, but when it succeeds it provides not only a legendary moment for the audience, but an opportunity that catapults me in a new direction.

If you feel constrained in your delivery it is likely that you need to take some calculated risks and vulnerably experience discomfort in trying new things. This might change not only how the audience sees you and how you see yourself, but also what you believe constrains you.

If you can experience discomfort until it becomes comfortable, stay in the moment with authenticity to connect with each audience, then you are well on the way to becoming a master of stages.

So, tread the boards boldly and expand your repertoire by adding new strings to the instruments that embody your show. It's time to step off the predictable stage and into the spotlight of your potential.

Chapter Summary/Key Takeaways

Performance is about awareness – of yourself and of your audience. This helps you ascertain what they will be open to receiving at that particular moment.

Extend your stage – it goes far beyond the dimensions of your perceived platform.

Each day/meeting/presentation/interaction is an opportunity for growth, experimentation, fresh approach, creativity.

Chapter Fourteen

Attitude and Leadership

Whether people like it or not, good salespeople in any business are looked upon as leaders. A person's title means nothing to me when it comes to Leadership, as those who influence and help in any industry are the real leaders. The rest, to be honest, are just managers.

I know many will be uncomfortable with this statement, but this is what I know after 30 plus years in sales.

To be a good leader, you must have a good attitude, and this, together with sound principles of Leadership make up what I call the top-performing people in a business who create excellent teams, who will follow them all day long.

While I was preparing to write this book, I came across the following on Leadership and attitudes, which I had been given many years ago and is still relevant today.

The Ladder of Success

Attitude	Success Level
I DID	100%
I WILL	90%
I CAN	80%
I THINK I CAN	70%
I MIGHT	60%
I THINK I MIGHT	50%
I WISH I COULD	40%
I DON'T KNOW	30%
I DON'T KNOW HOW	20%
I CAN'T	10%

The only choice you have now is to decide where you are on the ladder and what you need to change to move up the rung.

ATTITUDES

"The longer I live, the more I realize the impact of attitude on life. Attitude, to me, is more important than facts. It is more important than the past, than education, than money, than circumstances, than failures, than successes, than what think, say, or do.

It is more important than appearance, giftedness, or skill. It will make or break a company, church, or home. The remarkable thing is we have a choice every day regarding the attitude we will embrace for that day.

We cannot change the inevitable. We cannot change the past. The only thing we can do is play on the one thing we have, and that is our attitude.

I am convinced that life is 100% what happens to me and 90% how I react to it.

And so, it is with you.

We are in charge of our attitudes."

Author unknown

> ### *Key takeaway*
> - Attitude and Leadership go hand in hand.
> - Leaders are only as good as their team.
> - We choose the attitude we have on any day.
> - Managers tell people what to do; Leaders ask Can I help.
> - Be the leader you wish you had.

Principles of Good Leadership

Below is a list of what I consider are good leadership principles that I have observed during my life. I learnt the majority from average leaders and managers, as they have shown what not to do. I have come across leaders that make it look easy and natural, they have a presence when they walk in a room, and people will follow them no matter what. I encourage you to create your own list.

1. **Never be scared to make a mistake**
   The best leaders back themselves no matter what and own the results.

2. **Make sound decisions, not emotional decisions**
   The best decision is made without emotion.

3. **Use the strengths of your team to succeed and promote a sense of teamwork**
   A team is the sum of its members, so using the skills of team members builds trust.

4. **Know those who you lead and look after their welfare, and they will look after you**
   Knowing your team and being supportive creates a harmonious culture.

5. **Never shirk responsibility; accept it as nothing you are given you cannot handle**
   Showing you get everything that is given to you breeds confidence.

6. **Be prepared to lead by example**
   Monkey see Monkey do.

7. **Develop your team's potential**
   If you don't develop your team, they will look elsewhere.

8. **Know your strengths and weaknesses**
   The best captains and leaders know when and where to step up and when to leave the rest to those who do it better.

9. **Communication breeds trust, so keep everyone informed**
   Most issues are created by poor communication.

10. **Be honest, even if it is uncomfortable**
    The toughest one but being dishonest is far worse as one untruth can ruin a team in one go.

Chapter Fifteen

Virtual Selling

Covid-19 has taught us that we need to be adaptable and be able to pivot our businesses. Failure to adapt in business can be fatal. The same tactics, skills and the need to deliver value are still as important as ever but you need to offer them in different ways then what we used to.

Never has an industry been told that you need to keep doing what you are doing, but by the way, you can't do it the same way you have always done it. Many have thrown their hands in the air and walked away, saying this is all too hard; others have questioned how they can build a relationship with customers and build rapport when everything is digital or virtual.

News flash, everything you have read in this book is current, accurate and crucial. It is important that you transfer everything you have learnt and apply it to the new world we live in. Don't worry face to face sales will always be here, but there will be a portion of the market who will only want to deal with us digitally, and we need to cater to them.

While people and companies have reduced purchases in many areas, they are still looking to spend and have invested more money in online options, computer technology, and cost-efficient strategies. This has resulted in an expectation that anyone doing business with them have also lifted their game.

Virtual or Remote selling should now be part of every business structure and is as important as any other area in the sales chain. I listened to a person state that anyone over fifty years of age will struggle with the apps; this person was so out of kilter. I know a prominent Australian company that was launching a phone app for tradespeople to order their supplies while on the job site, to avoid the long waits of call centers. They asked their sales representatives to have customers from all demographics to beta test the app before launching it, to iron out any kinks.

To the total surprise of the IT gurus, the most significant uptake of the app was in the 40-60 age demographic; the younger demographic was the most resistant. The company had not researched who placed the orders in their customer's businesses and now had to rewrite the advertising and guides to reflect the target audience. This caused a very animated conversation in head office and resulted in a total strategy rethink.

Sales Funnels

What is this, you ask; well, put simply, imagine a funnel, the different levels represent a step-by-step process that tracks your customer's progress as they move closer to a purchase:

- Step 1. **Awareness**
- Step 2. **Interest**
- Step 3. **Decision**
- Step 4. **Action**

As your customer moves along the funnel, it gets smaller until it reaches the final stage where a customer is pre-qualified and makes the online purchase.

It will help if you use this model to storyboard your sales process to ensure that it works in the digital world.

Step 1. **Awareness** is where you promote your product, not sell, on as many media platforms you are aware that your customer uses. The adage of you cannot sell a secret is never any more accurate than it is today. When you build awareness and communicate just enough information about what your product does or solves it generates interest.

Step 2. **Interest** This is where your client dives a little deeper into the facts behind your offer and evaluates if what you are offering is what they need.

Step 3. **Decision** where you present your irresistible offer and lay your cards on the table.

Step 4. **Action** making the purchase process easy will get most sales over the line, followed by an automated email thanking them and provide information pertaining to delivery.

This can all be achieved without interacting with a client if your funnel is perfected. A great example of a funnel could be;

Facebook/Instagram advertisement with a short video, linked to your website for more information then attached to a buy now page.

One important note: always have the option for a client to be able to contact you during every step as this will give a sense of security and can save your sale if they need to communicate with someone.

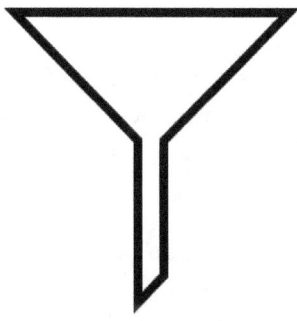

Podcasts

The 21st Century online radio shows, available 24/7. The best thing about these podcast shows is that you have the ability to advertise on those that you know your ideal customer is listening to. And at a far lower cost than other forms of advertising, or you could promote yourself by being a guest on one.

The advantage of being a guest is that you are seen as the go-to expert in that field, and the podcasts get played over and over, costing you nothing. All you are required to do is tell people where they can contact you at the end of the episode, and you can generate many new leads, plus you get to promote the podcast on your web page and social media pages, further expanding your reach.

If you prefer why not start your own podcast talking about your industry, sponsor your show and generate interest in your product and services that way. The possibilities are endless, and it is very easy to create your own podcast.

Video

Today, video has become a significant way of generating leads and interest in a product or service. The surprising thing is that anyone with a modern mobile phone can easily make, edit, and publish short information spots. The whole purpose of using video is to create awareness of your product, educate potential customers and entice them into making a purchasing.

Video can be used on all social media platforms, the content should be short and direct to the point, unless it is an educational video, then 15 to 20 minute maximum, loaded onto YouTube and linked back to your website or socials.

A video aims to tell a story in the shortest amount of time possible. **PIES** is an excellent framework to use when storyboarding your video: **Problem, Idea, Evidence and Solution**.

Problem Have you ever looked at a freshly painted wall and wondered how they got it to look so good in a short amount of time.

Idea I have found that every time I use a small cheap roller without a pole, I struggle to get the job done, let alone without any roller marks

Evidence Trade professionals will tell you investing in a quality roller on a sturdy pole will ensure an even spread of paint and allow you to finish the job much quicker.

Solution I took their advice and picked up this quality roller and pole set from our warehouse, and in no time, I had the lounge room wall at home looking great and the wife much happier. Remember happy wife, happy life. If you want to find out more about this or any other product, hit the link below to take you to our website.

You can adapt this framework any way you need to, as it is a quick way to generate leads for your business.

Websites

An easy-to-use website is essential if you want to convert leads to sales. Every page must be identified, modern in design, bright, and easy to read. Remember, by the time a customer arrives at your website, they are already interested in what you are offering and maybe just looking for some extra information to confirm what they already know.

Start with your Landing Page, which is a one-pager that contains all the important information and contact details, email and/or phone number. These are great to use while your site is being constructed.

Ensure you have a frequently asked questions (FAQ) section, as this will reduce the number of emails or phone calls you need to respond to. A great way to build the FAQ page is to list all the enquiries you have received over a six month period and then convert them to this page.

When you decide to upgrade to an entire site, keep it simple. Only have pages that are relevant and what your customer is looking for.

Too many pages will turn prospects off and lose you sales. People like to know who they are buying from, so having a page about you, the history of the business, what you stand for, and which charities or causes you support is very important to today's audience.

No matter where you are on the site, you must always have an "order now button" to short circuit the process for when a customer has made their mind up.

Creating a website can be done in a few ways. Some companies will host and give you a template style to build your own, and these are great when you are starting out. When you decide to move to the next level, shop around for the right fit of a web designer for you and the business. It is easy to spend thousands of dollars and end up with a dud.

Finally, remember you only have less than 30 seconds to grab their attention when they land on your page, so ensure your customer will like what they see.

Strategy

The whole idea of remote or virtual selling is to gain your customer's attention as quickly as you can and hold on to them for as long as it takes to convert them from browsing to purchased.

To enable this, you must ensure that the content you provide relates to what the customer is looking for, offers real value and a sales process that reflects how they purchase.

Depending on where they are interacting on the sales funnel gives you the information you need to know how close they are to a decision and will assist staff in how best to serve.

Automate as much of the process as you can, so that the basic tasks can be completed, this will then free up time for your staff to serve your customers. I always say, People buy People, regardless if the sale is face-to-face, virtual or in the digital space, you need to ensure that everything you do has a personal touch and that your site is easy for customers to navigate and use.

The easier the process the bigger potential for them to buy more and to recommend your business to others that prefer the digital side of sales.

Key Takeaways

- Customers are no fools, and most have done their research on what they want.
- Virtual sales are no different to face to face. It is just the medium of delivery that differs.
- You have less than 30 seconds to grab the customers attention.
- Every form of social media is an avenue to a customer.
- Know who your customers are before designing your sales funnel.

Chapter Sixteen

Close not Close

Most people believe that closing is the essential part of selling, I do not agree. Yes, it is a significant part of the process, but it is not the be and all end of everything we do. If you have done everything you possibly can along the sale process, then closing should happen automatically.

I have seen a customer close a deal themselves without much more prompting than a simple question from an employee.

In this chapter I will show you different techniques that you can use and other suggestions to be mindful of as we start to wrap up everything we have discussed.

The Soft Close

I call this the "Friends Close", no, not the TV Show but rather the style you use to gain trust and give a sense of deciding together. This is great to use with clients who are nervous about a purchase, and you have a genuine rapport with or the quiet client who likes to deliberate before a decision is made.

Shifting these types of customers towards a sale takes patience and acknowledgment every step along the way until you get to a time where there is nothing further to answer, and you can say, "Well, are we ready to make a decision now?" This makes them feel supported and secure along the journey and more likely to buy. It also means that they will be more open to your suggestions if you believe it will deliver a better result for them, and you.

The key to this close is to use inclusive words like, we, with a soft, thoughtful voice that shows excitement when you see them happy.

The Hard Close

Anyone who has bought a cheap used car or come across a less than an ethical person has experienced this type of close. The one where you feel pressured to buy, right now, as the offer will not be there, or my boss will change his mind if we do not do the deal now.

This type of close uses words that give the customer a sense of urgency if they do not act and can be used to ensure a person makes a rash or quick decision that if they don't, someone else will. This style was mainly used during the 80s and 90s before people became educated about this tactic.

There is no doubt, when used correctly it can extract a decision from a slow decision-maker and bring clarity to any underlying issues that have not been raised or discovered during the process.

A positive way to use a hard close is to ask questions like, "Have I answered all your queries today?" or, "Are you in a position to buy today? Is there anyone else we need to speak to before you decide? If not can we move forward with the purchase or purchase order today?" There is nothing wrong with pushing if you feel that there is nothing more to discuss, as it will give you a response either way. The skill is knowing how far to push because if you ignore their body language, you may go too far and, you will lose the sale.

When I have sensed that I had a timewaster in front of me, I have gone straight for the jugular and started to do a challenging close which resulted in them leaving, and I was able to focus on customers who valued my time.

The Suggestive Close

I believe this is what they teach in clothing store management, as they seem to have perfected the art of using suggestive words and actions to close a sale before we even realise it. It is a brilliant way to sell and close in one go in environments where purchases can be transactional, and the salesperson is time poor.

I have been told that the success rate of when you get a person to try a garment on versus just looking at it is at least 50% more. Add into that the comments of "That looks great on you" or when they agree with what you have said and kapow! It is all over.

Suggestive closing has been used for as long as sales have been around, and most do not pick up on it until after the fact. Start by asking a very open question so your customer can reveal exactly what they want. All you need to do is repeat the same information back differently, ask for confirmation and then say, "I have the perfect item you need".

In other situations, you can sit back and watch a person browse until they stop and show interest in an item. By just walking up slowly and saying hello, you will often be met with a comment about the item; by agreeing with the customer, you suggest that they are correct in their opinion, and in most cases, the sale is closed.

When you mirror words and phrases back to a customer, it reinforces what they have said and suggestively gives a sense of confidence to a purchase. A physical way to do the same is to take an item that the customer has said they wish to buy and hold it for them at the checkout. This suggests to the customer that this deal is now done, and you still want to buy more.

This same tactic can be used in any sales scenario just adapt to the service or product you are offering.

Hurry! Hurry! Hurry!

Everyone has seen the advertisements around the limited time offers that are only on sale this weekend. There are also the ones on social media about deals ending any day now that are unlikely to be repeated any time soon; oops, a few months later, the same advertisement reappears, must have worked, right.

If you can create a sense of urgency, you can increase the probability that a purchase will happen. I would never suggest that you tell an untruth or pressure someone who you know really should not buy, but it is a tactic used by just about every industry to get sales moving.

A real estate person will often tell you they have multiple offers in place, or a car yard will say that a model is hard to get, or that a price rise is imminent. Both statements are correct and will move a customer to decide either way, which is what you want. Sometimes a slight prod about an impending change to a condition of sale during the negotiation can be enough to make a client decide. This mostly works with people who procrastinate or use your tender to shop around to gain a better deal.

We can expand this sense of urgency to the FOMO theory, that's right one that is used every day based on the **Fear Of Missing Out**. So many people without realising it get trapped by this subconscious urge to buy something because others say it is good or they may miss out and feel left out of the crowd.

There are studies all over the world of what happens when a business puts a sign on a product stating "Our most popular line" or "Customer Favourite" even "Get in quick" that shows a significant increase in sales of the highlight product. This tactic can be used to move excess stock as it plays on the FOMO need.

There is a famous story from the USA where a local TV station decided to interview people waiting to buy the new Apple iPhone. The crew walk down the line and ask a lady, 23rd in the queue, if she had spoken to others waiting and had she made any friends. To the surprise of the reporter, she excitedly said that she was actually 25th inline and had done a deal with the lady ahead of her to switch spots in return for her $2500 shoulder bag. When asked why you would do such a thing she answered "I heard that this store did not have many of the new phones and I did not want to miss out" (I think both ladies got their phones).

The internal need to feel part of family is natural and can be used by the gifted salesperson to close most retail deals. When a person believes they will miss out on a deal of any type they will instinctively move to an emotional state to decide and then justify later with reason.

I am out of Here

A salesperson who is confident they have offered a good deal or considers they are being used is free to walk away from an agreement or meeting as much as anyone. I have used this tactic myself to significant effect.

There are those customers who will keep asking for more regardless of your offer, and others will use you as an unpaid consultant to get a better deal elsewhere.

I had dealt with a client, who had large contract on offer, that I had already meet with on two separate occasions. They kept asking me back for further meetings, I obliged for one last time to see where the deal was heading. I was kept waiting for 20 minutes, and then their representative pulled apart our credit application and offer, to be greedy and disrespectful to the company I worked for, which was larger than they were and had a standard of treating everyone equally, no matter the size. It would have been a terrific win for my figures; however, I would not lower my offer, let alone my standards

Closing is not always about winning the sale. It is also about walking away from customers that are not worth the time. In the end, with this client, after listening for 30 minutes on how good they were and what I had to change, I stood up and said thank you for your time, but it is clear to me that we were too far apart to make a deal. I will see myself out. I did glance back for just a minute to see the look on their faces, priceless.

I have walked away on other deals only to have them come back asking if they could take up the offer. When I walk away from a deal is not arrogance it is knowing that I have offered the best deal, and it is the company's loss for not accepting what was being offered.

If you don't ask, how will you Close

You can ask all the right discovery questions, follow all the verbal and non-verbal cues, give an excellent presentation, but what is the point if you don't ask for the sale.

Before you ask, confirm that you have negotiated a deal your customer is satisfied with. Both sides must be comfortable with the deal, and your client knows the value they are getting. Do not, I repeat DO NOT sound desperate or overexcited; remain calm as your client will pick up on this and ask for a discount. You could even spook them away, and you have wasted your time.

If you feel you need to give them a nudge, use a delaying tactic, keep them waiting while you check on availability under the guise of, "let me check when we are available next while you make your mind up". This creates a sense of urgency and upon return, they will be eager to hear your answer.

Face-to-face closing is always better than over the phone. It is harder for a customer to say no. Email or phone conversations typically lead to a lower result unless you have a long relationship with them.

If you feel you are ready to ask the question but need to gain control or power back, use the double back method. In that case, this is an easy way to give yourself a break, focus your thoughts by just saying, "Let me take a minute and call my boss to see what the best deal is today". Walking away gives you time and power and having a boss to call, even if this is not the case, it makes them feel important and gives you leverage. Returning with a statement like "I just spoke to my boss, and he has approved me to provide the deal as discussed plus a bonus of XYZ when you buy today". You can blame your boss about the deal closing today, if they are wavering, so you can get them to move forward.

No matter your style or tactic, it is all about moving your client to a point where you can ask the question. If you have built a great relationship with a client and met all their requirements, solved all the problems, delivered on what you have promised, you do not need to close in most cases.

When you have completed every step of the way, and you achieve a sale like this, it can be one of the most satisfying feelings.

Embarrassing Case Study

Writing this book has been like a window into the past with all the stuff-ups, wins, and near misses I have had along the way. (And that's just from a Friday night at the pub) To be honest, I do remember one of my first sales roles and being very excited about my new position. Being keen to impress, I threw myself at anyone I could to get a sale, and I think just by sheer numbers, I was succeeding, well I thought I was. One day I had the chance to pitch to a client that I had been hounding for months; excited and prepped, I followed my process, ticked all the boxes, and answered his questions.

I stood up, said thank you, and walked out on cloud nine. OOPS! I had forgotten the one thing that I needed to do the most, ask for the order. I had got so caught up in what I was doing that my mind was running quicker than my body could keep up. I walked past the receptionist and heard, Mr Elliott, I think Mr Walker is looking for you. I turned around, and there he was, he smiled and said, Rob, you had me 10 minutes into our meeting. Do you want our business, or should I look elsewhere? Thankfully he was a kind person who knew I was inexperienced and chose to save my bacon. I never forgot him for that and many years later I did the same for a person in the same position as me.

People are often sent into your life for a specific purpose, and it is up to us to open our minds to the lessons they teach us. Mr Walker was such a person.

Key Takeaways

- Closing is as much about tactics as a gut feeling.
- Use all your senses to know when to ask.
- Clarify you have answered all the outstanding questions.
- No can mean Yes, just later.
- If not now, then when.
- Create your own style of closing.
- If in doubt, ask.

Chapter Seventeen

That's a Wrap

I sincerely hope that you have enjoyed this book as much as I did writing it. The most important thing to remember is that every one of us is different. Our experiences and beliefs shape who we are and how we react to situations; the same can be said for our customers. Before I sign off, I have a few suggestions for you to consider.

Mentors

I believe that everyone should have access to a mentor when they start off to help them grow personally and professionally. They can be an experienced person in the business you are working for or someone you have created a strong relationship with that you trust and will be completely honest with you.

Coaches / Education

When I started there wasn't a lot of external education around to support me in my sales journey. You do not need to study long courses or have a coach for 12 months of the year, but the best in the industry all keep their knowledge up and have coaches call them out when needed. Technology, methodologies, and markets are evolving so quickly that you need to find ways to keep up with what is happening. Business networking and organisations, private training companies, and even local networking groups are great to tap into for information.

Coaches can be found everywhere; the most important thing is to find someone who has done the hard yards themselves and can help you discover the answers to your questions.

Final Message

When times get challenging, never lower your standards or go against what you believe in. I accepted a job with someone who I assumed was a friend and accepted the process of how I was given appointments and thought all was above board. It became apparent very early, that I was in front of potential customers under false pretences, not happy.

The product was great, but the employers' methods of gaining a sale were not, and I quit. We all have our own goals, standards, and ethics which we are responsible for, no one else. Set a standard and stick to it.

Have fun, I love selling and having a happy client, I encourage you to do the same. Celebrate your good days and cast aside the days that challenge you. Get up every morning with a smile and purpose, be grateful for everything our universe shows us.

Have a Groovy Day

Rob Elliott
SALES AND BUSINESS COACH

www.ingramcontent.com/pod-product-compliance
Lightning Source LLC
Chambersburg PA
CBHW071519080526
44588CB00011B/1495